I0023844

Thomas Lloyd

Lloyd's Pocket Companion and Guide through New York City for

1866-67

Thomas Lloyd

Lloyd's Pocket Companion and Guide through New York City for 1866-67

ISBN/EAN: 9783744755788

Printed in Europe, USA, Canada, Australia, Japan

Cover: Foto ©Andreas Hilbeck / pixelio.de

More available books at **www.hansebooks.com**

LLOYD'S

POCKET

COMPANION AND GUIDE

THROUGH

NEW YORK CITY,

FOR 1866-67.

PUBLISHED BY THOMAS LLOYD,

198 Water Street,

(Old U. S. Hotel Building,)   NEW YORK.

NEW YORK:
TORREY BROTHERS, PRINTERS, 13 SPRUCE STREET.
1866

CONTENTS.

WHY IT WAS WRITTEN.

INTRODUCTION.—Arrival of Jonathan Griggs. Jonathan wants to see New York 7

WALK THE FIRST.

ON BROADWAY.—The Battery. Castle Garden. Emigrants. Bowling Green. Trinity Church. An Impostor. Jonathan purchases a new hat. The Crossing Sweeper. St. Paul's Church. Astor House. City Hall. Stewart's Store. An Accident. New York Hospital. Pearl Street. Carter, Kirtland & Co's. A Dinner at Taylor's Saloon. The Arrest. Billiard Tables. St. Nicholas Hotel. Prescott House. The Diamond Palace. Metropolitan Hotel. Sewing Machines. Jonathan Buys a Carriage. History of an Inventor. Gurney's Gallery. Stewart's Retail Store. Union Square. Steinway's Pianos. A visit to the factory. Fifth Avenue Hotel. Madison Square. General Scott. Hoffman House 11

WALK THE SECOND.

CENTRAL PARK.—Jonathan late. Hours the Park is open; its size, location and names of the various gates. The Mall. The Lake; Swans, Venetian Gondola. Music. Croton Reservoir. The Roads. The Trees. Remains of Military Fortifications. A Menagerie. Play Ground. Jonathan Sleepy. Skating Pond ... 59

WALK THE THIRD.

PAGE

PUBLIC AND BENEVOLENT INSTITUTIONS.—The Tombs : cost
of keeping a prisoner. Custom House. Bulls and
Bears. Sub-Treasury. Post Office. City Arsenal.
Five Points. House of Industry. Astor Library.
Cooper Union. Mercantile Library. New York
University. Bible House. Historical Society. Free
Academy. National Academy of Design. House
of Industry and Home for the Friendless. Institu-
tion for the Blind. Deaf and Dumb Asylum. Mag-
dalene Female Asylum. Orphan Asylums. Jew's
Hospital. St. Luke's Hospital. Children's Hospi-
tal. University Medical School. College of Physi-
cians and Surgeons. Medical College. Medical In-
stitute. Medical Dispensaries. Bellevue Hospital.
Blackwell's Island and its Hospital, Penitentiary,
Alms-House, Work-House and Lunatic Asylum.
Randall's Island. Where to obtain permits to visit
Blackwell's and Randall's Islands 70

WALK THE FOURTH.

NEWSPAPER OFFICES.—Jonathan ahead of time. A Fare
Wanting. The Missing Fare accounted for. Circula-
tion of New York Papers. *Tribune, Times,* and
Herald. A visit to the *Times* Office. Torrey Brothers'
Printing Office. Subterranean Establishment—Din-
ner Hour. A Great Country 89

WALK THE FIFTH.

PUBLIC AMUSEMENTS.—Academy of Music. Irving Hall.
Wallack's Theatre. Winter Garden. Olympic
Theatre. Barnum's Museum. Wood's Theatre.
Broadway Theatre. Bowery Theatre. New Bowery
Theatre. New York Stadt Theatre. Negro Min-
strelsy 98

WALK THE SIXTH.

PAGE

WHARVES AND SHIPPING —Camden and Amboy Railroad.
Bethel Ship. Savannah and New Orleans Line.
Jersey City Ferry. Washington Market. Hoboken
Ferry. Erie Railroad. Albany Boats. The Cali-
fornia Line. The Steamship *Arizona*. Oyster Boats.
Liverpool Line. How Kindling Wood is made.
Bishop's Derrick. Manhattan Gas Company. The
Offal Boat. Across the East River. Hunter's
Point Ferry. Novelty Iron Works. Webb's Ship
Yard. The *Dunderberg*. A Representative Ameri-
can. Italian Marble. Dry Docks. Fulton Market.
Dorlon & Shaffer's Oyster Saloon. Farrar & Lyon.
Franklin Market. Brooklyn Ferries. North Ameri-
can Lloyd Line to Bremen...................... 102

WALK THE SEVENTH.

CHURCHES.—Baptist. Congregational. Dutch Reformed.
Friends. Jewish Synagogues. Lutheran Methodist
Episcopal. African Methodist Episcopal. Methodist
Protestant. Presbyterian. United Presbyterian.
Associate Reformed Presbyterian. Reformed Pres-
byterian. Protestant Episcopal. Roman Catholic.
Unitarian. Universalist. Miscellaneous. Missions. 126

HINTS FOR REFFERENCE.

CARRIAGE FARES.—Banks. Insurance Offices. Post Office
Guide.................................... 147

ILLUSTRATIONS.

	PAGE
HOFFMAN HOUSE, (Frontispiece,)	.
CARTER, KIRTLAND & Co.'s STORE	27
INTERNATIONAL HOTEL	31
PHELAN & COLLENDER'S BUILDING	35
BALL, BLACK & Co.'s	41
METROPOLITAN HOTEL	43
WHEELER & WILSON'S BUILDING	45
STEINWAY & SON'S WAREROOMS	53
STEINWAY & SON'S MANUFACTORY	57
THE BIBLE HOUSE	77
STEAMSHIP "CONSTITUTION"	115
UNITED STATES LUNCH ROOMS	123

WHY IT WAS WRITTEN.

I will introduce myself. Reader, my name is John Wetherby. I was born in Greenwich Street, near the Battery. At that period Greenwich was a far different street to what it is now. Then, many of our leading merchants had their residences there. However, we have not to do with Greenwich Street, beyond the fact that I was born there.

Neither would I have mentioned that, if I had not wanted to show that I am a native of New York City, and to the manner born. I have grown with its growth, and there is not a nook or corner on the whole Island of Manhattan that I am not familiar with.

I am now a hale, hearty old man of—— But no! There are some secrets a man keeps locked up within his breast. Suffice it that I am a tolerably old man, and have never been absent from the city more than a month at a time since my birth.

Walking is my delight. Often, stick in hand, do I start out of a morning, and roam about the whole long day, viewing the various places of interest, and noting down in my memory any curious or quaint story.

I have said walking is my delight. So also is it my pride. I am proud that I can still out-walk many a younger man.

A nephew of mine, who was brought up in an Eastern city, once paid me a visit, but I walked him off his legs in no time. On the second day he protested against so much walking, and actually wanted to hire a carriage.

I sternly declined such a conveyance. I told him that Nature had given us legs to use, and we ought to use them—not keep them cooped up under the seat of a carriage.

It was no use talking to him; so I let him have his own way, but positively refused to accompany him. Subsequently he regretted this, for, without a guide, he left the city very little wiser than he came.

This, it must be confessed, set me thinking ; and I thought of the many strangers that visited New York and departed in the same condition as my nephew.

" Why not," I pondered, " write a Guide of the goodly City of New York ? "

The idea grew strong upon me. So I determined upon writing one that would be equally useful to the resident or the transient visitor, whether viewed while riding or afoot.

It was evening. I had just partaken of my supper, and ensconced myself in my easy chair to read the evening papers, when I heard a carriage drive rapidly up to my door.

"That can be nobody for me," I muttered. But that assertion was seemingly contradicted by the door-bell being violently rung.

" Who can it possibly be ? I expect nobody. Some one has mistaken the house." So I turned once more to my newspaper.

In a few minutes my hired girl entered the room, and told me a gentleman was down stairs in the parlor who wished to see me.

"A gentleman! That can't be," I said, somewhat foolishly it must be owned.

" Yes, sir, it can," she replied ; "he said he wanted to see Mr. John Wetherby, and that's your name."

" Well, well, tell him I'll be down directly," and I commenced putting on my coat and boots, for when interrupted I was taking mine ease in dressing-gown and slippers.

On entering the parlor I discovered that my visitor was my old friend Jonathan Griggs, whom I had not seen for years.

" Why, Jonathan ! " I exclaimed.

" Why, John ! " he ejaculated.

And we seized one another's hands and shook them so warmly that it would have done you good to have seen it.

" When did you arrive ? " I asked, as soon as I had recovered sufficient breath to put the question, for the hand shaking had been so hearty that it partook somewhat of violent exercise.

" Only just now. As soon as I got off the cars, I called a carriage and drove to your house."

" That's right. If you hadn't done so, I would never have forgiven you. You stay with me, of course ? "

" If you have any place to put me."

" Any place to put you ! Jonathan, you shall have the best room in the house. A room, did I say ? While you are here, the whole house is yours, and at your disposal."

" The same impetuous John Wetherby as of old," said Jonathan, smiling. " I shan't want the whole house, John, but I will accept a room in it."

" Then the affair is settled. Where is your baggage ? We must send for it at once."

" It was on the carriage at the door, but, by the bumps I heard in the hall just now, I imagine the hackman guessed I was going to stay here, and has deposited it there already."

This supposition was soon verified by Mary entering the room and stating that the coachman wanted his fare.

After Jonathan had been shown to his room, and he had cleansed himself of the dust and grit of travel, we sat down to spend a comfortable evening and talk over old times.

Dear me ! I have been so busy receiving Jonathan Griggs that I have almost forgotten to introduce him. It is an oversight almost unpardonable, but I will now strive to make amends.

Jonathan is now a large farmer out West, owns ever so many thousand acres, and is one of the largest corn and cattle raisers in the whole State of Illinois.

He went out there when he was quite a young man—properly speaking, he was only a boy—and by his energy and industry made himself what he is.

That is now over thirty years ago, and this was his first visit to New York since his departure. Consequently, he was as much a stranger in the city as though he had never been in it.

" We sat long into the night, and it was with a feeling of reluctance we parted to take the rest we both needed—but Jonathan more than I, as he had been traveling.

In the morning, after we had partaken of breakfast, to which we did ample justice, I asked my friend Griggs how long he intended to remain in New York.

"A week. Then I have to visit some friends down East."

"Only a week! Why, you can't see New York in a week."

"That's all the time I can spare; so I must make the best of that. I place myself under your guidance, and you must show me as many of the sights as possible in that time."

"Can you walk?" was my only reply to this.

"My dear John, what a question! I am as robust and as healthy as ever, and you know in my younger days I was no mean pedestrian."

"That's sufficient. Come, let us be off at once;" so, taking our hats and sticks, we sallied out, arm-in-arm, to view the sights and see the lions of New York.

WALK THE FIRST.

BROADWAY.

"This," said I, as the stage deposited us at the extreme end of Broadway, "is the Battery."

"Indeed," replied Griggs, who was all eyes and ears ; "but where are the cannons?"

"Cannons," I exclaimed ; "this is not a battery proper, but only bears that name. That round building on the edge of the water is called Castle Garden."

"I have heard of that before. When Jenny Lind came to this country, she made her first appearance there ;" and Griggs was delighted at his knowledge.

"True," I replied ; "it was one time a fortification, but now it is devoted to more peaceful pursuits, being used as an emigrant depot."

"Is that where all the emigrants land ?"

"Yes, every one of them. It is an excellent institution, and saves many a poor person from being robbed of all they possess in the world."

"How ?"

"In former times the emigrant, as soon as the ship touched the dock, was dumped out upon the pier like so much merchandise, and made to shift for himself the best way he could. Sharpers were on the watch for him ; he was robbed and cheated in every direction ; and in a few hours he had not a cent left to bless himself with."

"Poor fellow! How terrible it must be. In a strange country ; no friends ; no home ; and robbed of your all !"

"That is altered now. As soon as the emigrant arrives here, he is at once taken in charge by the Commissioners of Emigration, who watch over and care for him as though his interests were their own. If the emigrant wishes to go East, West, North, or South, his railroad ticket is procured for him, and he is started toward his destination without the expenditure of an unnecessary cent."

"And what do the Commissioners of Emigration charge for their trouble?"

"Nothing. The people of the Empire State pay for the protection of the poor emigrant, and it is their pride to do so."

"A most excellent institution."

"It is indeed. Many a poor foreigner has had reason to say the same."

"What is that little inclosure?"

"That is the Bowling Green."

"Do they play bowls there?" asked my friend Griggs.

"No, not now; but before the Revolution it was used as such."

"There is a fountain there," said Griggs, delighted as a child at the jet of water that was spirting up.

"Yes; and where that fountain now stands was once a leaden statue of George III., which, at the commencement of the Revolution, was torn down and moulded into bullets."

"How interesting! What a number of omnibuses! Gracious, they seem endless. It appears to me that everybody must ride in New York, or else they would never want such a number of stages."

"Some people walk," I replied, laughing, "as you will see before we finish our peregrinations."

"How many omnibuses are there, do you know?"

"Yes, I do. There are nearly seven hundred stages that go up and down Broadway daily. Each one, on an average, makes ten trips per diem. A trip is the journey down and up again. This makes it equal to the employment of seven thousand stages daily for the use of our citizens."

"Dear me! And do they all pay?"

"Indeed, do they. Besides these, there are several car lines, all of which are more or less crowded, and which I will tell you about in course of time."

"What church is this?"

"The Church of Trinity. It is the oldest church on Broadway. That street opposite is Wall Street. In it are the Cus-

tom House and the Treasury building, which we will visit ono
of these days.''

"Can we enter this church?"'

"Certainly. Every visitor to New York should do the
same ; ascend the steeple, and there view the city which lies
stretched out like a map at his feet."

Our ascent of the steeple was a work of some little difficulty,
for both Griggs and myself are not so young as we once were ;
and though we can hold our own with many a younger man
upon level ground, stairs and ladders have a tendency to make
us breathe somewhat hurriedly.

But our exertions were amply repaid by the beautiful sight
that met our gaze, as we looked out from our giddy height
upon the world below. Beneath us lay the city, which now
appeared in all its vastness and power. No one who has not
viewed the Metropolis of the Western World from an elevated
position can form an adequate idea of its greatness.

"As we look beneath us," said I to Jonathan, "and see
the busy throng hurrying to and fro, hither and thither, each
bent on his own particular business and the accumulation of
wealth, and then cast our eyes upon the stores and warehouses,
many of them filled to depletion with the products of every
nation upon the face of the earth, brought hither by those
very ships we now see fringing the shore, we can scarcely believe that a little over 230 years ago the whole of this island
was purchased of the Indians for a sum equivalent to twenty-
four dollars. Yet so it was."

"No! Is that so? A mighty good speculation."

"And now its estimated value is between seven and eight
hundred millions.''

Jonathan could only gape at me open-mouthed with astonishment.

"In this city over two hundred miles of paved streets have
already 'been surveyed and laid, leaving room for over one
hundred more streets not yet projected."

"How large is the city?" queried Jonathan.

"From the Battery to Harlem Bridge is eight and a half
miles ; the area, twenty-three square miles."

" A wonderful city, truly."

" Wonderful, indeed. Destined at no late day to be the
foremost city in the world—though, perhaps, not rich in historical association and buildings, rich in energy, tact, and commercial enterprise that will soon place it beyond the reach of
foreign rivalry."

Jonathan made a motion as if to speak, but, apparently
seeming to think better of it, he refrained ; so I continued :

" On the right, Jonathan, if you will look through this little
window, you can see our justly celebrated and beautiful Bay,
dotted with the vessels of every clime. Beyond that are the
Narrows ; and, stretching far away in the dim distance, may be
seen the delightful Highlands of Navesink."

" How far, or rather how extended a view, can you obtain
from here ? "

" About twenty miles. But come, if you have enough of
this, let us get down "

So saying, we proceeded to the floor below, in which are the
chimes, the finest in America. Pointing them out to Jonathan,
he wished to know why there were so many bells, and stated
that at home, in the part of country he came from, one bell
was sufficient to ring the people into church.

" Certainly," I said, " one bell is enough to summon
people to church, but one bell can never ring out such music
as these."

" Music ? " echoed Griggs.

" Yes. On all holidays the bell-ringer peals out the most
delightful music, comprising such tunes as ' The Star-spangled
Banner,' ' Hail Columbia ! ' ' Yankee Doodle,' ' The Last
Rose of Summer,' and other melodies of a like nature."

" How I should like to hear them."

" And so you could if you were in the city on Washington's
Birthday, the Fourth of July, Christmas Eve, or New Year's
Day."

" What a pity it is I can't be," and Jonathan heaved a deep
sigh.

When we had once more reached level ground, and were
shown the beautiful chancel service of silver that had been

presented to the church by Queen Anne, we went to look at
the exterior, and view the monuments that have been erected
to many illustrious men, such as Alexander Hamilton, Commo-
dore Lawrence, and Lieut. Ludlow.

On the north east corner of the churchyard, just facing
Broadway, a very fine monument, in an architectural point of
view, has been raised to the "Sugar House Martyrs," and.
those American patriots who fought and fell in striving for
and obtaining our National Independence.

"Is Trinity a very old church?" asked Griggs.

"It is the oldest church in the city. The first building was
destroyed by fire in 1776, and rebuilt in 1790. This second
edifice was pulled down in 1839, and the present noble structure erected. It was finished and consecrated in 1846."

"How high above the level of the street do you think we
ascended?"

"About two hundred and fifty feet."

"No! I never was up so high before. That will be something to talk of when I return home. Why, my neighbors
will scarcely credit it;" and Griggs was evidently delighted at
the surprise he intended giving his friends.

"The extreme height of the steeple is two hundred and
eighty-four feet; length of the building one hundred and
ninety-two feet; breadth, eighty feet; height, sixty feet."

"What a memory you have!"

"I told you I knew New York pretty well. But let us be
going; we have more sights to see."

As we left the church, Griggs, who was a little in advance,
was accosted by a man all grimy with coal dust, carrying upon
his shoulder a shovel and a basket. To him this man told a
most piteous tale: how he had been sick for over twelve
weeks, and in the hospital, leaving his sickly wife and six
young children totally unprovided for. He was now trying to
earn a few cents by carrying in coal, but up to that hour he
had been unsuccessful. Griggs' heart opened in a moment,
and, putting his hand in his pocket, was about bestowing alms
upon the man when I arrived upon the scene.

"What are you doing, Jonathan?" I asked.

"This poor fellow here is in great want. He has a wife and six children, and has been sick himself. Let us give him something, John."

" I will not give him a cent," I replied ; " and if he does not immediately be off, I will give him in charge of the police."

" Why, John," exclaimed Griggs, with a look of horrified surprise, " how can you be so cruel ? "

"Cruel! Not at all. Look how he slinks away at the mention of the word policeman. That man, Jonathan, is an impostor."

" Goodness gracious—an impostor ? "

" Yes ; he has been about the city, playing that same old dodge, for years."

" You don't say so ? " ejaculated Griggs, opening his eyes with astonishment; " I was just going to give him some money."

" I saw you were. But, Jonathan, it would be a safe plan, and the most judicious, not to give a cent to any beggars. When you feel like giving away money in charity, give it to some public institution, not indiscriminately in the street. The Commissioners of Charities and Corrections are especially appointed by the city to look after and relieve the deserving poor."

" That is a very good idea. I will do as you suggest. During my stay in New York, whenever I feel like giving money away in charity, I will put the amount I intended giving in a sepa-rate pocket, and when I leave will send it to that institution I think most needs it."

" A capital idea. If every one were to follow your sugges-tion, there would be fewer beggars to importune or annoy people in their walks."

Jonathan Griggs became so enthusiastic and elated over this proposition of his that he paid no attention to where he was going, and as we were crossing Cortland Street I was alarmed and startled by seeing him floundering and scrambling under the very feet, apparently, of a horse attached to a dray.

His hat was knocked off and trampled in the mud and mire of the street, his cane lay in the gutter, and he himself was performing some of the most curious gyrations ever before attempted by any staid, respectable old gentleman on Broadway.

The driver quickly pulled up his horse, and in another moment I had Griggs, panting and breathless, on the sidewalk.

"Are you hurt?" I anxiously inquired.

"No, no," responded Griggs, cautiously feeling his arms and legs to see if he was uninjured ; "I don't think I am ; but it somewhat frightened me."

"And no wonder, for it frightened me also, and I was not struggling with a horse. How did it happen ?"

"Well, John, I really don't know ; but I think it was all my fault, as I was not looking where I was going."

Jonathan Griggs' hat, which had been picked up and handed to him by some of the passers-by, was in a most deplorable state. It was crushed out of all shape, and almost unrecognizable from mud. His clothes were also bespattered, and it was absolutely necessary he should be brushed off before we proceeded on our walk ; so, taking him across to the Howard House, at the corner of Broadway and Maiden Lane, I requested the boot-black of that hotel to make Jonathan again presentable, which he speedily did. But his hat was beyond redemption. There was a big indentation in the front, and a slit extending from the crown to the rim had been made in the back. Passing again into the street, we soon found that Jonathan's battered hat was attracting great and universal attention. Many were the remarks made upon it, and many were the titters given as we were passed by, some unruly boys even going so far as to ask Jonathan who was his hatter. This could hardly be wondered at, for, to say the least, it did look somewhat curious to see a man, otherwise respectably attired, adorned with such remarkable head gear.

"John," queried Griggs, "don't you think the remarks made about hats are applied to me ?"

"Yes, Jonathan, I think they are ; indeed, I might say, though not wishing to hurt or wound your feelings, I am sure they are."

"You don't say so ! I was laboring under that impression myself. John, I must buy a new hat. Where can I get one ?"

"I will show you. The man I'm about to take you to is the hatter of all hatters. His styles set the fashion in New York, and you can safely say that every well-dressed, stylish-looking man you meet wears one of his hats."

"You don't tell me! Where does this celebrated hatter live, and what is his name?"

"He lives at 210 Broadway, corner of Fulton-street, and his name is Knox?"

"Why, I have heard of him out West."

"I have no doubt; but here is the store."

So, entering, Jonathan was soon fitted with a becoming hat from the varied and extensive assortment always kept on hand by Knox.

"It is astonishing," said Jonathan, "how a decent hat adds to the appearance of a man, and makes him satisfied with himself."

"A trite and true remark," I responded.

As we crossed Broadway, opposite St. Paul's Church, in order to obtain a view of the new building now being erected at the corner of Ann Street and Broadway, by James Gordon Bennett, the proprietor and editor of the *New York Herald*, and to be occupied, on its completion, for the transaction of business and publication of that influential journal, a little crossing-sweeper, broom in hand, importuned me for a penny. As I was about to give her one, Jonathan, laying his hand upon my arm, stopped me with—"Why, how's this? I thought you told me never to give anything to beggars?"

"So I did. But this girl is not a beggar; she works for what she asks for; she is, you might almost say, a necessity; by keeping this crossing clean, she helps to keep my feet dry and my boots unspotted. 'The laborer is worthy of his hire;' so I give her a penny."

"Quite right, too," ejaculated Griggs; "I did not think of it in that light;" and the kind-hearted fellow dropped a dime in her hand.

"This," said I, facing Jonathan round to look at the edifice corner of Broadway and Vesey Street, "is St. Paul's Church."

"Oh! yes," chimed in Griggs, always ready to impart what

little information he possessed of New York, "I know ; General George Washington attended Divine service at this place of worship after his inauguration."

"Yes ; quite right ; I see you are posted on some of the historical events of New York "

"I have read a little about New York," said my friend Jonathan Griggs, stiffening himself up, and blushing like a girl at the compliment I paid him ; "but what entablature is that?" he asked, pointing to a small slab of marble inlaid on the front of the building.

"That," said I, "is in commemoration of the gallant General Montgomery, who fell at Quebec during the Revolutionary struggle. St. Paul's is also famous for two other monuments—one of Robert Emmet, the Irish patriot ; the other, of George Frederick Cooke, the eminent tragedian."

I would here mention that strangers visiting New York invariably want to know the height, length, and breadth of every building ; so, imagining, and correctly, my friend was no exception to the rule, I continued :

"St. Paul's Church is 151 feet high, 73 feet wide, and the extreme elevation of the steeple is 203 feet."

"My goodness ! you know everything." exclaimed Jonathan, clapping his hands together with mingled admiration and surprise.

"No, not everything," I returned, smiling ; "but there are few men living who are more thoroughly acquainted with New York City as it is than I am."

"That I most readily believe. But what is that large granite building on the opposite corner ? "

"That is the Astor House, the largest and best hotel down town. It has been built twenty-six years, and has received within its walls as guests some of the most distinguished men of modern times. It can accommodate now over 600 guests at one time."

"Quite a little town in itself, I declare," murmured Griggs.

That's so. Let us enter for a few seconds and take a look at the rotunda."

So we ascended the steps and entered the room, situated on the ground floor, that bears that name.

" Here," I continued, " the thirsty can bibulate and the hungry can be fed (if their impecuniosity is not too great to prevent them), even if they are not guests of the house."

" It is a handsome and commodious room," said Jonathan, gazing wondrously around him ; "and the frescoes on the ceiling are quite pretty, too."

" Yes, the house throughout is well appointed and fitted up. But come ; time flies ; let us be getting farther up town."

Once more in the street, Jonathan Griggs, wishing to see the height of the building, backed himself into the street, and for the second time that day nearly made a Juggernaut sacrifice of himself by being crushed by a passing vehicle.

Rescuing him from this second danger, I told him—somewhat petulantly it must be confessed—he must certainly be more careful for the future, or I most positively would not accompany him if he insisted on risking his life and limbs in such a reckless manner.

He was all apologies in a moment, and as penitent as a chided child. So sorry did he appear, that I regretted having said a word, and turned the conversation by pointing out to him the City Hall and its surrounding park, situated just across the way.

" The City Hall Park," I commenced, in my character of showman, " contains about eleven acres. That white building which you see at the northern end of the inclosure, is the City Hall, in which the City Fathers are supposed to dispense justice, of which that figure perched on the summit is the emblem."

" And there is a fountain here, too, same as on the Bowling Green."

" Yes ; but this one is generally dry, though occasionally it does give a few spasmodic squirts. In former days, strangers and visitors from the country were often fleeced by sharpers when they attempted to enter any one of the park gates. One of these scamps would accost the stranger and demand money for admittance, which the stranger, not being accustomed to the ways and manners of New York, would incontinently pay.

" The scoundrels ! " vehemently exclaimed Jonathan Griggs,

casting a suspicious look around and hastily buttoning up his pockets.

"But, thanks to the efficiency of the Metropolitan Police, such petty ways of extortion are never heard of now."

"And are your police good?"

"Good? Taken as a whole, there never was a finer body of men in the world. Even foreigners praise our police system; and New Yorkers may well point with pride when they see them marching in platoons up Broadway."

Here Jonathan pulled out his watch to compare it with the City Hall clock, and inquired if the latter was right.

"New York time is governed by that clock. I presume that every man who possesses a watch, and whose business is down town, regulates his timepiece by it. It originally cost $4,000."

"Four thousand dollars!" ejaculated the astounded Griggs; "a good price for a clock."

"True; but then it's a good clock for the price. The main wheels of it are two feet six inches in diameter, and the pendulum-bob weighs three hundred pounds."

"Gracious goodness! Three hundred pounds!" muttered the astounded Jonathan.

"The works of the clock," I continued, "are not immediately behind the face, as many suppose, but in the story below, and are connected with the hands by rods twelve feet in length."

Jonathan Griggs lifted up his hands in mute surprise.

"The building itself was commenced in 1803, and finished in 1810 In it are the Mayor's offices, the Common Council's, and several others, all intimately connected with municipal affairs"

"What is that unfinished building behind intended for?"

"That, when finished, is to be the new City Hall. It is larger and more commodious than the present one, and, owing to the rapid growth and increase of the city, was found absolutely necessary in order to facilitate the city's business."

Jonathan, apparently thinking he ought to say something, mumbled, "Indeed!"

"The corner-stone," I went on, "was laid in 1862, and there is no doubt that 1867 will see the completion of the building."

"That," said I, as we crossed Chambers Street, pointing to the white marble building on the opposite side of the street, "is one of the largest wholesale dry goods establishments in the world."

"Whose house is it?"

"Alexander T. Stewart's. You see it runs the whole length of the block, and extends some distance down Chambers and Reade Streets, which are on either side. Besides this, he has one equally as large up town, which was expressly built for the retail trade."

"He is very rich, is he not?"

"Rich! I presume he is one of the richest men in New York City. The tax he pays upon his annual income is enormous. I am afraid to tell you how much it is, lest I should not be believed."

"But I would believe you," said Jonathan, eagerly.

"Would you?" I asked, assuming a doubting tone.

"How foolishly you talk, John. Have I ever doubted your word?"

Seeing he was taking seriously what I only intended for a joke, I told him:

"The man who knows everything, and whose memory is so excellent, has really forgotten the amount of tax Alexander T. Stewart does pay. If he had not, he would have told you in the first instance"

"You don't tell me! I really thought you imagined I would doubt your veracity. How stupid of me;" and Jonathan laughed loud and long at his obtuseness.

"It is an excellent plan," I continued, "when in conversation you come across any startling fact you are not quite sure of, or have forgotten, to say in an off-hand manner, as I did just now, 'If I were to mention it, I should not be believed.'"

If Jonathan laughed loud and long at his own obtuseness, he laughed louder and longer at what he was pleased to term my adroitness.

"Can you find out, John?" he asked; "I really should like to know the income of such a man as Stewart.

"I can and will. Before you leave, I will tell you the tax paid upon the annual incomes of several of our Merchant Princes."

"Thank you. That will be another very interesting item to carry away with me."

"When Stewart first commenced business," I went on, "he determined to mark his goods at a fair profit, and to make no abatement under any circumstances whatever."

"A most judicious plan."

"So it proved. In those days it was no uncommon thing for ladies even to haggle over their purchases, both buyer and seller trying to get the best of the other."

"That was not a judicious plan."

"No; Stewart saw at once it was not; so he determined upon altering it, and has reaped his reward by now being worth his millions."

As we were talking, there was of a sudden a loud cry of warning, followed by one of terror, and right in front of us we saw a poor old man knocked down by a passing vehicle, the wheel going clean over his body.

In an instant, as if by magic, the body of the man was hidden from view by the gathering crowd. A policeman soon appeared, hailed a passing carriage, and placed therein the injured man in order to convey him to the New York Hospital.

We followed.

Jonathan was all sympathy, and was anxious to learn the extent of the man's injuries.

Knowing the resident physician, we had no difficulty in obtaining admittance, which otherwise we should have done, as, very properly, the crowd is always excluded.

If, when an accident happened, all who followed the injured person to the hospital were admitted, the movements and operation of the surgeon would be greatly impeded, and the excitement upon the patient seeing so many people around him would be extremely injurious, and might result fatally.

Learning that the only injury the man had sustained was a few external bruises and a slight scalp wound, we left.

Upon doing so, Jonathan immediately overwhelmed me with questions concerning the institution, which I at once endeavoured to satisfy.

"The New York Hospital," I commenced, " situated, as you see, between Duane and Worth Streets, and exactly opposite Pearl, was founded by the Earl of Dunmore, who was then Governor of the colony, in 1771."

"Then it was originally founded by an Englishman?"

"Yes ; but it did not receive its first charter until 1776, nine days after the Declaration of Independence."

"Thus leaving Americans to finish what an Englishman begun."

"Just so. With only an annual revenue of sixty-one dollars and sixty cents, the New York Hospital has to depend mainly up n voluntary contributions."

"And is no charge made to the sick or maimed?" queried Jonathan Griggs.

"Yes, a charge of five dollars per week is made for females, and six dollars for males ; but the patient for that sum nas the best of nursing and the best of medical attendance."

"It must do an immense amount of good," said Jonathan.

" It does. The ground upon which the hospital stands is extremely valuable, and, if sold, would realize sufficient to build and support a hospital, without any extra aid, further up town."

"Then why not sell it?" asked Jonathan.

" For this reason : this is the only hospital down town, and many a poor injured creature's life has been saved by receiving prompt surgical attendance here, who would have died had they been carried to any hospital away up town. The Board of Governors know this, and prefer paying any deficiency in the expenses out of their own pockets to risking the life of a human being."

" Do you know how many patients they receive here yearly?"

" From three thousand to three thousand five hundred. For those afflicted with contagious diseases, separate apartments are provided."

"A very proper precaution."

"Most decidedly. It also possesses a theatre for surgical operations, besides other apartments necessary for so large a hospital. The building is one hundred and twenty-four feet long, and the two wings are fifty feet deep."

"And what a splendid approach to the building," exclaimed Jonathan, admiringly.

"Yes, indeed. The avenue is ninety feet wide, and a double row of trees stand sentinel from the entrance gate to the very door of the hospital."

"And splendid trees they are, too," said Jonathan, gazing upward at their gnarled and weather-beaten limbs.

"Seven miles from here," I continued, " is a branch hospital of this. It is for lunatics, and is called 'The Bloomingdale Lunatic Asylum.'"

"What a terrible place it must be."

"No ; there you are mistaken. Everything is as light, airy, and as pleasant as possible. Nothing that can alleviate the suffering of the poor demented creatures is left undone. All the surroundings are cheerful, and, though a place of confine- ment, the chief end and aim of the physicians is to make the place comfortable, and as much like a home as possible."

"I see I was mistaken ; but my idea of a lunatic asylum was a gloomy, sombre place, like a tomb."

"So it is most people's. The building is two hundred and eleven feet long, sixty feet deep, and four stories high. From the roof a most delightful view of the surrounding country can be obtained."

"How terrible to lose one's reason," said Jonathan, more to himself than me ; and he was lost, apparently, in melancholy thought. Rousing himself at last, he asked what street that was opposite the hospital.

"Pearl-street," I replied ; "and they say that the man who laid out that street did it in a very extraordinary way."

"How was that?" asked Jonathan, pricking up his ears, and all agog in a second to hear anything in the shape of a story.

"The other end of this street is about a mile down Broadway; and of all the sinuous, tortuous thoroughfares in the wide world, I believe there are none to equal it."

"Is it crooked?"

"Crooked? Crooked as a ram's horn. Well, the legend has it, the surveyor, wishing to lay out this street, started a cow in the morning, and in the evening he followed the track the lactaceous bovine had made, and staked it out for a street."

"On that site," said I, pointing to the large wholesale clothing house of Carter, Kirtland, and Co., situated at No. 340 Broadway, between Worth and Leonard Streets, "once stood the Broadway Tabernacle, famous—"

"Oh! yes, I know," said Jonathan, eagerly interrupting me; "Deacon Johnson, when he once made a visit to New York, on his return told me all about it. He came on to attend the May anniversaries, and said they were held in the Broadway Tabernacle."

"Right. So they were. But the mutations of a great city have transformed it into an immense mercantile house, with marble front, the largest of its class in the world."

"What business is carried on there?"

"A business," I continued, "that is one of the largest and most important on this Continent. Over one hundred firms are engaged in it in this city, of which Carter, Kirtland, and Co.'s is the representative house."

"But you have not told me the nature of the business."

"I am speaking of the wholesale clothing trade, in which, in this city alone, a capital, probably, of over twenty millions is employed."

"So large a trade must necessarily give employment to a great number of work-people."

"It does. Residing in this city and vicinity, there are about ninety thousand operatives, who receive as wages upwards of thirty millions of dollars. This firm has facilities for employing from 5,000 to 8,000 good hands."

"You surprise me."

"So large a house, to be properly organized, requires as many as five or six partners in order to thoroughly oversee and supervise every department of the business. The firm consists of

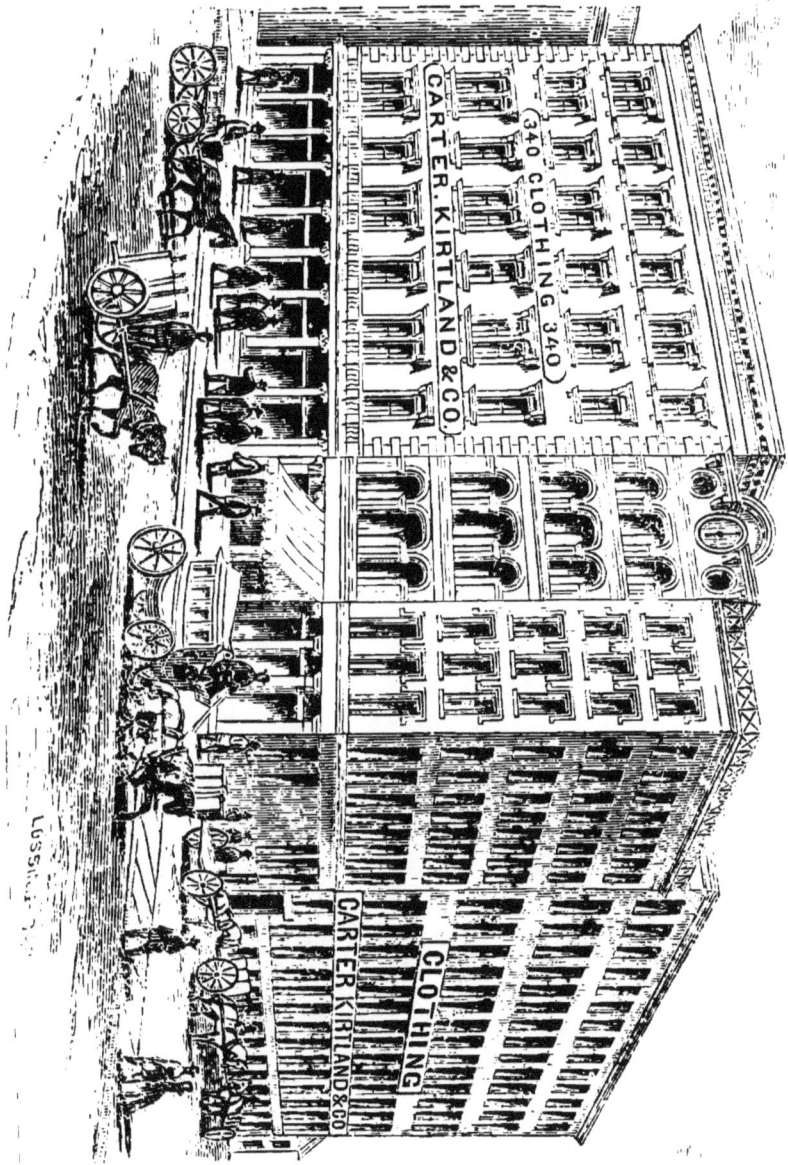

CLOTHING
CARTER KIRTLAND & CO

340 CLOTHING 340
CARTER KIRTLAND & CO.

Messrs. Samuel Carter, William H. Kirtland, Charles B. Peet, John Rose, and John H. Werts—gentlemen who have been identified with this branch of business for many years past, and whose acquaintance ranges through nearly every State and Territory in the Union."

" So large a house I should like to inspect. Can we do so?''

"Certainly," I replied ; and entering, we made known our wishes to a gentleman who came forward to receive us.

The first floor, which has a frontage of 30 feet on Broadway, and extends back 200 feet, with an extension on Worth Street and Catharine Lane of 100 square feet, is used as a salesroom, in which are piles upon piles of ready-made clothing in endless variety. On the second floor is the cutting department, connected with which is the modeling room, where the designs and patterns are conceived and prepared. The third floor is devoted to the cloth room, where all productions, domestic and imported, intended for manufacture, are taken, and subjected to a rigid examination by a competent and experienced inspector.

We were also informed that none but the most skillful operators are employed, and that, in point of material, durability, and finish, their goods are in all respects equal to custom work.

"That I can readily believe," said Jonathan, taking up some articles and examining them, " for no man could wish to wear better articles of dress than these."

" And that seems to be the opinion of their customers," said I, " for I am told that this house does business to the extent of a million and a half dollars per annum."

Leaving this building, we soon arrived at Franklin Street, on the north east corner of which is located Taylor's Saloon. The upper part of the building is used as a hotel, named the International.

' Quite a handsome saloon," whispered Jonathan to me, peeping in at the door

" Yes, and a commodious one, too. I presume it is the largest one of the kind in New York."

" So I should judge But look at the floor. It is inlaid

with variegated marble. And how handsomely the whole place is fitted up!''

"It is, and must have cost a good round sum to have so decorated it, as that floor you are now looking at contains an area of seven thousand five hundred feet."

"You don't say so!''

"But I do; and in the saloon below there are accommodations almost as ample."

"My gracious! Are all the tables ever filled?''

"My dear fellow," I replied, pitying his ignorance, "the tables are always full. It is an accident when you see them empty."

"Really, now!''

"It is the favorite resort," I continued, warming with my theme, "of the fashion and *elite* of New York, and strangers never consider they visit the city unless they make a call at Taylor's."

"John," said Jonathan, grasping my hand, " we must dine here some day."

"That we will," I replied, returning the pressure; "and if you find in any place better fare or attendance, I'll——I'll forfeit a hat."

"One moment, John," said Jonathan, stopping me as I was moving onward; "I have an idea ; you may not credit it, but I assure you that I have."

"Well, Jonathan, and what is it?'' I asked, laughing.

"When I was a boy, I was told there was 'no time like the present.' Acting in that belief, let us dine here to day."

"With all my heart. My walk has made me hungry, and I feel I could do justice to the excellence of Taylor's viands."

On entering the saloon, Jonathan was at once struck with the gorgeousness and Oriental magnificence of the interior ; and when I told him that the cost for embelleshing the ceiling alone cost $3,500, he was filled with awe and wonderment.

Seating ourselves at one of the marble tables that was covered with a cloth rivaling newly-fallen snow in whiteness, we were waited upon by a polite and attentive attendant, whose sole end and aim in life appeared to be to give us pleasure.

It took a long while to order our dinner, and I am afraid we must have taxed the patience of our waiter most severely, but he was too well trained to show it, for Jonathan was so perplexed with the extent and variety of the bill of fare, that it was extremely difficult for him to choose.

"Why," said Jonathan, when the waiter had departed to give our order, "they seem to have here every known eatable and drinkable in the universe."

"Yes," I replied, "the luxuries of the world are always at the command of the guest ; every delicacy that can be brought to New York being promptly and liberally supplied by the proprietor."

"And the prices are not high ?"

"Indeed they are not. A dinner at Taylor's may be rendered as economical as the most prudent can desire, or as extravagant as the requirements of a *gourmand*."

Further conversation was cut short by the arrival of our meal. Jonathan holding that no man can do two things at one time ; when he eats he cannot talk, and when he talks he cannot eat. So our prandial repast was devoured in silence.

When we had finished, and the demands of the cashier satisfied, Jonathan expressed a desire to see the kitchen and other auxiliaries of so extensive an establishment.

Making known this wish to the cashier he at once referred us to Mr. Taylor, whom we found in his private office. This gentleman immediately acceded to our request, and lead the way to the culinary department and store rooms.

The kitchen was as clean as a new pin, and the various utensils appertaining to the *cuisine* were as shining as polished silver. Those not in use were ranged along the walls. each hanging upon its allotted peg, as the motto of this house is "a place for everything and everything in its place."

Next we were shown the butcher's shop – larger than the average of such shops in the city ; the poultry store ; the bakery ; the vegetable room; the milk room ; the grocery ; the laundry ; and, though last not least, the wine vaults and segar room.

Everything was in apparently endless profusion, and on
our expressing surprise at so large a quantity of stores being on
hand, we were told that their store rooms, extensive as they
are, could not hold more than a couple of days' supplies. The
segars and wines, however, had been stored for years.

We were next shown the up-stairs portion of the building,
which is set apart for Hotel purposes, called, as I have said before, the International.   The whole is replete with comfort,
being elegantly furnished, and with bath rooms and other con-
veniences on each floor.

" There is an old saying," said I to Jonathan ' that there is
nothing like leather,' which is verified by the handsome and extensive establishment of W. A. Ransom & Co., just across the way.

" Are they in the leather business ?"

" They are in the boot and shoe trade, and their house is the
largest and oldest in the United States."

" Indeed !"

"It is situated on 384 and 386 Broadway, between White and
Walker streets.   The building is of white marble, and is 175
feet deep, and 45 feet wide."

" The business houses of this city are certainly of palatial
proportions," remarked Jonathan.

"They are indeed.   The house of Ransom & Co. was established in 1820, and has been successfully carried on by different
members of that family ever since, and during forty-six years
have only changed their place of business three times."

"That is somewhat remarkable for an American house of
business, is it not?"

" It is.   But it has great advantages. The members of the
firm are so well known throughout the trade, and buyers so
well satisfied with them that in many instances the amount of
goods wanted to be purchased is simply given, and the selection left to the firm."

"Such a system must be of great benefit to country merchants."

" And country merchants seem to think so.   For this house
is constantly shipping goods to all parts of the United States."

" And the territories as well, I presume."

INTERNATIONAL HOTEL, Broadway, cor. Franklin Street.

" You are right. Besides which they are constantly export-
ing goods to the West India Islands and South America."

" Americans have occasionally to look after the understand-
ings of foreigners," said Jonathan slyly.

Seeing that he expected me to laugh at this terrible joke of
his, I did so, evidently, much to his satisfaction.

Passing Canal Street, Griggs and myself sauntered leisurely
up Broadway, he admiring the various stores and the goods exhibited for sale in the respective windows.

" I imagine," said Jonathan, " that here on Broadway a
man can obtain everything he wants. Let him make known
his wishes, whether an article of luxury or necessity, and he
can be supplied without leaving the street."

" I guess you are right. As the Cheap Jacks say, anything
can be procured, from a needle up to a locomotive."

" What a splendid store !" and Jonathan Griggs pointed
admiringly at the dry goods establishment at the corner of
Broadway and Grand Street.

" Yes, and an ornament to our street."

" So it is. Who are the proprietors ?"

" Lord and Taylor."

" What a business they appear to be doing !".

" Their house is one of the largest for the retailing of dry
goods in New York, which you will readily imagine when I
tell you that the building cost three hundred thousand dollars."

" No ?"

" A fact, I assure you."

At this juncture, and before Jonathan had recovered from
the surprise he had been thrown in by my informing him of the
cost of the building, a quiet, determined-looking man stepped
up to him, and in a bland, courteous manner, inquired :

" Have you lost anything ?"

" Lost anything ! What do you mean ? No !" And Jonathan hurriedly slapped his pockets to see if they were safe.

" Excuse me," said the man, " I am a detective ; and seeing
some young pickpockets hovering around you in a suspicious
manner, I thought I would ask you. You are sure you have
lost nothing ?"

"Quite;" and Jonathan again went through the pantomime of slapping his pockets.

"Jonathan, your watch chain is loose," I told him, as I saw that article of dress dangling from his button-hole.

"Gracious me! so it is; and, John, my watch has gone."

"Ah! I thought you had lost something," said the detective; "wait here a moment;" and he darted away from us, and was lost in the crowd.

"I wouldn't lose that watch for a thousand dollars," excitedly exclaimed Jonathan; "it was given me by a dear friend of mine, who has since died. How careless of me, to be sure."

In less than a minute the detective returned, leading by the arm a decently-attired young fellow, whom he briefly told us was the man who had taken Jonathan's watch.

"I assure you I am innocent," said the accused. "Do I look like a thief?"

"No; I cannot say you do," replied Jonathan, quite bewildered.

"But I know him to be one," chimed in the detective, "and one of the most expert of Broadway thieves; so, come along with me to the station-house and prefer a charge against him."

Leading the way with the culprit, we followed, Jonathan bewailing his loss, and unwilling to believe so respectable-looking a young man could be a thief.

"If he should prove to be innocent," remarked Jonathan to me, "I should never forgive myself. Having an innocent man dragged through the street like a felon! Oh! it's terrible."

"But, Jonathan, the detective says he's a thief, and you may depend upon it he has good grounds for so saying."

Further conversation was cut short by our arrival at the station-house. The charge was made, the man searched, and, to Jonathan's surprise and delight, the watch found in his possession.

"How wonderful!" ejaculated Griggs; "the loss of my watch known to a stranger before I, the owner, was aware of it; the thief locked up; the watch returned to me; and all in less than twenty minutes!"

" Quick work," I said.

" New York is a wonderful city, truly. Though the tempo-rary loss of my watch annoyed and worried me at the time, I am not sorry it was stolen, for it has given me an experience that I otherwise would not have had."

" That is so ; but be more careful for the future. Your next experience in the same line may be more dearly bought."

" By not recovering the article stolen, do you mean ? "

" Just so."

When we had regained Broadway, and were continuing our journey up town, I pointed out to Jonathan, Mechanics' Hall, 472 Broadway, near Grand street. In it is a library, contain-ing about 16,000 volumes, for the use of apprentices.

Leaving Broadway for a few minutes, I said to Jonathan Griggs, " we will pay a visit to th establishment of Messrs. Phelan & Collender the largest billiard table manufacturers in this country or in Europe."

" Nothing I should like better," replied Jonathan. " But is the head of this firm the celebrated billiard player, Michael Phelan ?"

" He is none other ; and has done more toward elevating the game of billiards making it a refined and intellectual accom-plishment, than any other man in America."

" You don't tell me !"

" Not more than twenty years ago the delightful pastime of billiards was looked upon by the many as immoral, and voted, by the fair sex, as low. Now, no gentleman's house is con-sidered complete without a billiard table, and ladies and child-ren alike indulge in the recreation."

" But who wrought this change ?"

" Who, but Michael Phelan. He by his integrity and up-right bearing, showed that the game of billards was not neces-sarily associated with ill-breeding and ungentlemanly conduct, and has reaped his reward by now being looked up to as one of the leading business men of this city."

" Such a course is one to be repaid in good time."

" But here we are at the manufactory," said I stopping before the buildings, situated at No's. 63, 65, 67 and 69 Crosby street, between Broome and Spring streets. "It is five stories high, and is looked upon as the best appointed factory of its kind in the world '

Entering, we were at once received by the prompt, courteous, energetic executive member of the firm, Mr. W. H. Collender, who showed us the various objects of interest in the building.

Jonathan, who is a regular Yankee, in the matter of asking questions, immediately wanted to know how many men were employed.

" About one hundred and fifty ; we could employ more, but the capacity of our present factory will not admit of it."

" How many tables do you make yearly ?"

"Between eight and nine hundred, but that number is hardly sufficient to supply the demand made upon us for them."

" Goodness gracious !" exclaimed Jonathan, " I should never have thought there had been so large a sale for them."

" The great secret of our success is our combination cushion. It is made of one solid substance with three degrees of density, has, comparatively speaking, a solid face, and an elastic back, yet inseparable, and is insensible to injury by the concussion of balls. This permits an accurate calculation in regard to the rebounding force, and the scientific principle of angles, thus rendering the player less liable to err in his calculations."

" I play a little at billiards myself," said Jonathan, "and I know such a cushion must be of incalculable value."

" It is. This is the machine for making balls ; it is patented, and is, as you see, of most peculiar and ingenious construction. It is exclusively owned and used by us. By it each ball is made to a mathematical nicety, as round as possible for them to be made, and not one deviates a hair's breadth from the other."

" Do you make cues on the premises, also ?" asked Jonathan.

"Oh, yes ; and our stock kept on hand, both imported and home made, is the largest in the world."

" Are all the tables you make sold in this country ?"

" Dear me, no. Our tables are in demand and sold in Cuba, South America, China, Japan, British America, and throughout the whole of Europe.

PHELAN & COLLENDER'S BILLIARD TABLE MANUFACTORY,
Nos. 63, 65, 67 & 69 Crosby Street.

" Where will not American handiwork go to !" said Jonathan astonished.

" Beside, all the leading hotels in the principal cities of the
Union are furnished with our tables ; indeed, so popular have
they become, and so great the demand for them that they are
acknowledged by the public generally as the standard billiard
table of Ame ica."

Having thoroughly examined the bui'ding, and admired the
elegance and finish of the different branches of work, we withdrew, much pleased with our visit..

On our return to Broadway, the first building that attracted
Jonathan's attention was the St. Nicholas Hotel, located between Broome and Spring streets. To his many questions I
replied :—

"The St. Nicholas Hotel was erected in 1854, at a cost of a
million dollars. It is built of white marble, and is of the Corinthian order of archit cture. It has a frontage of 300 feet
on Broadway, and has accommodations for 600 guests."

" Immense !" was all that Jonathan said.

" As a security against fire, a large water-tank is fitted on the
top of the building, which is sufficient to deluge the whole
place in less than five minutes."

"Under this hotel, the St. Nicholas," I informed Jonathan,
" is a branch of one of the oldest drug houses in the city. I
allude to the firm of Hegeman & Co."

" Why, we passed a druggist's store, of that name, some
distance down Broadway."

" True ; so we did. And as we get further up, you will pass
some more of the same name. There are five houses of that
name in this city. At least, when I say five houses, I mean
five stores, as the whole of them belong to the same firm. The
principal house is situated at No. 203 Broadway ; the branches
of this parent house are at 399, 511 and 756 of this, the same
great street, and on the corner of Fourth avenue and Seventeenth street.

" It is a very handsome store," said Jonathan.

"So it is ; indeed, this firm is celebrated for the beauty of
their stores. They are also famous for the superior quality of

their drugs, medicines, &c. Purchasers may rest assured that all articles procured of them are genuine, and the purest that can be obtained."

" In case of sickness that is a great desideratum."

" They are also noted," I continued, " as being the first manufacturers of Medicinal Cod Liver Oil, and for which they have an enviable reputation throughout the whole of the United States."

" Out West," said Jonathan, " Hegeman's Cod Liver Oil is regarded as the standard medicine for all pulmonary complaints."

" Mr. William Hegeman," I continued, " the senior partner, gives the benefit of his long experience to the superintendence of the business ; everything that is bought or made, passes under his careful supervision."

" The eye of the principal is almost always necessary to insure success."

" That is a true and trite remark. The different stores are under the charge, either of junior partners or assistants, who have been brought up by them and who have had from fifteen to twenty years experience in the business."

" A most excellent plan," ejaculated Jonathan.

" The motto adopted by this house for the guidance of subordinates, is, never to send anything out of the establishment that is not perfect in every respect. It is needless for me to add, that strict adherence to such a course, has met with the success it deserves."

' Of that I could not have a momentary doubt; it would have surprised me had it been otherwise."

At this juncture a number of beautifully stuffed animals in the window of a fur store, opposite the St. Nicholas, attracted Jonathan's attention, and nothing would do but he must cross the street to view them.

We did so, and found it was the store of F. W. Lasak's Son, No. 520 Broadway. Jonathan was evidently well posted on the subject of furs, and related to me several little adventures, in which he figured conspicuously as a trapper.

At last, espying some splendid Russian sable, he entered the

store to examine it. He was received by a polite and gentle-
manly salesman, whom he overwhelmed with questions.
Had he been a Yankee, instead of a Western man, his inter-
rogatories could not have been greater.

He soon found that the stock of this house comprised the
richest Russian sable, Royal Ermine, Hudson Bay sable, Mink,
Oriental Lamb, as well as all other kinds of furs, including the
lower grades, such as Water Mink, Jennett, Coney, and in fact
all kinds of goods connected with the fur trade.

" You keep manufactured goods on hand?" he asked.

" Oh, yes ; our business is both wholesale and retail, but our
principal trade is the latter."

" And I can most positively asseverate," I chimed in, " from
personal knowledge, that they have always on hand a full and
complete assortment of manufactured goods."

" We also make to order goods of any desired pattern,
whether for ladies or gentlemen's wear "

" Your house has been established some years—has it not?"

" Since 1823 ; and our long and successful business career is
a sufficient guarantee that purchasers can rely upon the repre-
sentations made by our house, and that their confidence will
not be misplaced."

We were also of that opinion, and after Jonathan had told
another little story about a fox and a trap, we thanked our informant, and retired.

" Is that a hotel, on the opposite corner?" asked Jonathan.

" Yes ; that is the Prescott House, named in honor of our
great American historian. In point of architectural beauty it
is unsurpassed by any other building on Broadway."

" It certainly is very handsome."

" The entrance hall, with its beautiful frescos and tesselated
pavement, is one of the finest in the country."

" That I can readily believe," said Jonathan, looking in at
the door, admiringly.

" The furniture is of the most elegant, costly and comfortable description, the majority of it having been made expressly
for this house in London and Paris."

" You surprise me."

" The chief guests of the house are Europeans, who, upon arriving here in the steamer, at once proceed to the Prescott House, and make that their headquarters. And within its hospitable walls there is always some foreigner of distinction."

" That church opposite, situated at 548 Broadway, is the Rev. Dr. E. H. Chapin's, the celebrated Universalist preacher."

" Here, at 563 Broadway, is the music store of Mr. Thaddeus Firth, successor to the late firm of Firth, Son, & Co. His father, senior member of the firm, was for 45 years the head of the most influential music house in New York."

" Forty-five years! Almost a lifetime," ejaculated Jonathan.

" True. And his son, keeping pace with the march of the times, intends maintaining the excellence of the house to that standard obtained by his predecessors. It will continue to be the popular music house, both in the wholesale and retail department."

" Among the many splendid and costly edifices," said I, " erected on Broadway, none is more imposing than the lofty marble palace of Messrs. Ball, Black & Co., at the corner of Broadway and Prince street."

" It is a beautiful structure!" and Jonathan looked with unfeigned admiration upon the building.

" Constructed," I continued "of East Chester marble, it presents an ornament at once striking and beautiful, and may well be called ' The Diamond Palace of Broadway.' "

" And is that the name it bears?"

" Yes. But let us enter. The members of the firm will be glad to see us, and will give us a cordial welcome. The porch, through which we are now passing, is built in the Corinthian style of architecture ; the doors are imitation ebony, relieved by sandal wood and bronze."

" What large windows !" exclaimed Jonathan.

" Each one measures nine by fifteen feet, and were manufactured expressly in France, for this building."

" You don't tell me !"

" As we enter the vestibule what a beautiful scene is present-

ed to our gaze, momentarily bewildering us by the dazzling
display that breaks upon our view."

"That is so ; it is like fairy-land."

"The floor is of Italian marble ; the counter of the same material and richly carved ; the ebony colored cases around the
room filled with most beautiful and costly goods. On either
side are diamonds, amethysts, rubies, sapphires, emeralds,
onyxes, and precious stones of every description. Every hue
is represented ; every degree of brightness sends forth its charm,
and the bewildered eye of the spectator is fairly dazzled by the
beauty and splendor of the various gems."

"You are quite enthusiastic, John," ejaculated Jonathan.

"Enthusiastic ! and who can help being so, in such a place as
this ! Look at the ceiling ; see how beautifully it is painted to
harmonize with the whole ; on either side see what elegance
and taste has been exhibited ; behold the finely wrought cabi-
net work, and finely executed bronze candelabras with which
this floor is lighted, and then say if you can be surprised at my
enthusiasm."

"No, John, I cannot be surprised ; to tell you the truth, I
feel a glow of enthusiasm myself."

At this juncture one of the junior members of the firm, a
most genial and courteous gentleman, approached us, and we
at once placed ourselves under his guidance.

The basement floor of the building is used for a packing
room, and the manufactory of gas fixtures. One portion of
this room is divided off into a sort of cage, forming a burglar
proof safe 40 by 25 feet, in which can be placed from 1,200 to
1,500 plate chests, and other valuable articles entrusted to the
firm for safe keeping. Under the sidewalk on the Prince
street side, is the boiler room, where steam is generated in a
boiler of thirty horse power, for the purpose of driving machinery and heating the building. A steam engine of ten
horse power, furnishes the motive by which the machinery in
the manufacturing department is driven. A donkey engine
operates an elevator capable of raising six thousand pounds,
which communicates with each of the upper floors.

Passing through the main floor, we are led up stairs over a

flight of marble steps, fringed with ebony rails, and wainscoted with the same material, relieved by occasional ornaments of sandal wood, polished and finished in exquisite style. At the foot of these stairs are two life size bronze statues, elegantly and artistically finished. To attempt to give a description of these rooms into which we were led by these stairs, would be worse than u eless. Such an agglomeration of beauty, magnificence, wealth and taste, can not be equalled anywhere. Paintings and engravings of the most costly kinds ; statues and statuettes, in silver, gold, glass, wax, cork, bronze, plaster and stone ; ornithological groups combining taste with elegance ; illus- trations of natural history as rare as beautiful ; clocks and watches of every conceivable style of finish, from France, Eng- land, Germany and other parts of Europe ; Italian paintings, sculpture and engravings, of the most ancient as well as of the most modern schools—all these articles of vertu, with thou- sands of others, are scattered around in the best arrangement, but with a profusion truly wonderful.

The upper stories of this building, which is six stories in height, are devoted to the manufacture of jewelry and silver ware. The facilities for the manufacture of everything relat- ing to precious metals, are immense ; indeed, there are no more extensive workshops, in the whole country, than Messrs. Ball, Black & Co.'s, having room for and frequently employing three or four hundred men at one time.

The building is entirely fire proof, and so satisfied are the firm of this, that they do not insure any portion of their own goods. Though those articles of plate and value, deposited with them by gentlemen visiting Europe or the country, are insured to their full worth. This is simply done to satisfy the depositors. Often property to the value of many millions is de- posited with them.

It is also proof against the incursion of burglars ; the ar- rangements for their detection being exceedingly ingenious and perfect. By means of a patent clock, and the services of ac- tive watchmen—six of whom are in the interior of the build- ing, and two out—the most daring burglar would be foiled on every plan of attack he might make on the store. The

iron doors are fitted by a kind of lock which would defy all the ordinary force to move one of their tongues from its place.

The building is one hundred feet on Prince street, and fifty two feet on Broadway ; its height is ninety-eight feet from curve to cornice, and one hundred and twenty feet from base to apex. The average cost of the building was about $150,000. Now, with the present high price of materials and labor, it could not be built under nearly treble that sum. It is of the Corinthian style of architecture. On the summit of the building there is a golden eagle, about eight feet high, and measuring the same length from the tip of his wings ; it has served as a sign for this firm for the past forty years.

Before leaving the establishment, the gentleman who had kindly escorted us through the building, led the way to a private office, and there exhibited to our astonished and delighted gaze some diamond sets valued at $30,000 and $50,000 each.

"Do you ever sell such expensive sets?" asked Jonathan.

"Certainly," said our informant, smiling at the question ; "or we should not make them up. In former times when a salesman sold to the amount of a thousand dollars, he thought he had done a big thing, and would consider himself master of the situation, for that day, at least. But now a sale to the extent of a thousand dollars is an ordinary occurrence, and causes no comment whatever."

Thanking our guide for his courtesy, we withdrew, much pleased and gratified with our tour of inspection. Upon reaching the street Jonathan asked me how long the house had been established.

"It was founded," I replied, " by Erastus Barton in 1810, and the entire capital then invested by him was about equal to a day's profits at the present time."

"That I can readily believe."

"It shows what industry and energy will do. Perseverance, combined with integrity of purpose, will tell, and sooner or later will crown a man with success."

"That brown stone building," said I, pointing to the edifice

on the north-east corner of Prince street and Broadway, "is the
Metropolitan Hotel.   It extends through to Crosby street, and
covers two acres of ground."

" It.is a noble-looking structure, truly," said Jonathan.

" You are right; it is.   As an item of interest I would tell
you, that there are over 12 miles of gas and water-pipes running through the buildings."

" You astound me."

"There are many things that astound," said I, somewhat
sententiously, " in New York city."

Jonathan emphatically agreed with me.

" Here," said I to Jonathan, " at No. 575, is the fashionable
boot and shoe store of Mr. E. A. Brooks, who is celebrated for
the excellence and elegance of his work."

" Now," I remarked to Jonathan, as we neared 625 Broadway,
" we will take a look at the greatest invention of modern times."

" The greatest invention of modern times!" exclaimed
Jonathan, surprised ; " what do you mean ?"

" I mean what I say ; in fact, I am not sure if I said the greatest invention the world ever saw, I should not be more correct."

" You don't tell me ; what invention is that ?"

" I mean the sewing machine—one of the marvels of these
later days."

" You are right ; it is a great invention."

" And has done more good, and more to alleviate the suffer-
ings of poor overworked humanity, than almost any other invention you can name, and in many departments of industry,
has wrought a complete change.   Tailors, dressmakers, shirtmakers, hatters, shoemakers, clothiers, harness-makers, um-
brella-makers, and in fact, all business and trades, where sewing
is required, have been benefitted."

" You remember Hood's poem of the ' Song of the Shirt ?' "
asked Jonathan.

" Indeed I do : a more touching and beautiful poem was
never written in the English language.   If the sewing machine
has done nothing else, it has improved the condition of poor
seamstresses, and now it cannot be said that shirtmakers are

   "' Sewing at once, with a double thread,
      A shroud as well as a shirt.' "

"There are several makers of sewing-machines, are there not? Whose machine do you consider the best?"

"It is universally conceded, both by families and manufacturers, that Wheeler & Wilson's bear the palm. They are indorsed by such men as Henry Ward Beecher, Solon Robinson, the Rev. Dr. Vinton, and many other equally well known gentlemen, all of whom hailed the advent of a sewing-machine in their houses as a blessing. But here we are at Wheeler & Wilson's store."

Entering the front door, Jonathan was at once struck with the immense depth of the building, and the beautiful and elegant manner in which the store and warerooms were fitted up. The whole of the wood work, comprising the cases, desks, counters, staircase, &c., is of black walnut, oil-finished, and ornamented with carving and ebony moulding, making the *tout ensemble* perfectly delightful.

One of the most interesting things shown us, was the first machine ever made by Messrs. Wheeler & Wilson. It was constructed in 1851, and has been in use more than fourteen years. Compared with the machines of to-day, it is a cumbersome-looking affair enough, though in its day was considered remarkably handsome. Its original cost was $125—a much superior article can be obtained now for $55.

"I presume your sales are much larger now than then," said Jonathan.

"Slightly so," replied our informant; "in 1853 we sold 799 machines; now we are manufacturing them at the rate of 50,000 per annum."

"It seems almost incredible.'

"It will not, when I tell you, that there are many establishments in this and other cities, that have four or five hundred sewing-machines for the use of their workpeople. In New Haven there is a house that employs 400 of the Wheeler & Wilson machines for making shirts alone. A shirt made by the machine, takes one hour and sixteen minutes in the making; so you can imagine, that in the course of a week, there are quite a large number of shirts turned out."

"Has the introduction of sewing-machines injured needle-women to any extent?"

"On the contrary, they have been greatly benefitted; new branches of needlework have been introduced, and the old ones greatly extended, giving the operator better remuneration, and lighter and more healthful work. Many owners of sewing-machines earn from $50 to $100 per month."

"Why, the smallest amount is a small fortune to many needlewomen."

"True. The sewing-machine has become almost a necessity; no family or manufactory where sewing is required to be done, is complete without it."

"It must be more healthy than the cramped and stooping posture of the old style of sewing?"

"The hygienic importance of the sewing-machine is not second to its commercial; the unhealthful nature of needlework is proverbial. The cramped posture, the strain of the eyes, the derangement of the digestive organs and the nerves, over a monotonous task, have told, with telling effects, upon the health and character of needlewomen."

"How many hands do you think your machine is equal to?"

"About ten. Sewers accustomed to make by hand thirty or forty stitches a minute, are surprised at the facility with which the machine accomplishes so much, and come to look upon operating on the machine as an agreeable pastime, rather than work."

"How many stitches can the machine make a minute?"

"From five to six hundred, according to the material and quality of the work; when driven by steam-power, fifteen hundred, and two thousand stitches a minute are not an unusual average."

"My goodness! it seems almost incredible."

"It does; but it is, nevertheless, a fact. One great feature in the Wheeler & Wilson machine, is the wide range of its application. For instance, a person furnished with one of those machines, can employ them in making shirts, mantillas, diamond ruffling, skirts, hats, caps, &c; in fact, it sews all materials, from the stoutest woolen to the finest cambric; consequently, as long as sewing is to be done, the machines are sure of something to do."

WHEELER & WILSON'S BUILDING, 625 Broadway.

" Do these machines make button-holes ?"

" No ; but they do almost everthing else. Garments are made entirely by it, with the exception of sewing on the buttons ; laces are stitched on ; folds, tucks, gathers, plaits are laid and stitched ; cord run in ; binding put on, and quilting can also be done after elaborate and beautiful designs."

" It is certainly wonderful."

" We have a button-hole and eyelet-hole machine, which is capable of making 100 button-holes per hour."

" Astonishing !" exclaimed Jonathan, as we bowed to our guide, and made our exit from the building.

" On the corner of Bleecker and Mercer streets," said I, " is the establishment of Messrs. Lindeman & Sons, the inventors and manufacturers of the new Patent Cycloid Piano Fortes, which they claim have a superiority of tone, a more beautiful form, and will stand in tune longer than any of the old style of instruments."

" And what hotel is this?" asked Jonathan, when we had arrived opposite Bond street.

" This is the La Farge House," I responded. " It is built of white marble ; seven stories in height, and capable of accommodating between four and five hundred guests."

During our walk up Broadway, Jonathan had been admiring the various stylish and elegant equipages that crowded that thoroughfare. As we neared Fourth street, a splendid Clarence Carriage, with a full circular front of plate-glass, drawn by a couple of bays, dashed by us. This set us talking about fast horses, carriages, wagons, and all things else appertaining to the road. Jonathan said he wanted to purchase a carriage and set of harness. and asked me the best place to do so.

'· You could not have spoken at a more opportune time, for just across the way, at No. 10 East Fourth street, are the carriage and harness warerooms of Mr. John C. Ham ; we will go there and look at some carriages, and if you cannot be suited, you will be hard to please, as he constantly has on hand about 150 different styles."

" Is Mr. Ham celebrated as a maker ?"

" Indeed, is he. Unlike most of the principals of other firms, Mr. Ham is himself a practical mechanic, and supervises

the make and finish of each vehicle turned out of his fac‑
tory."

" Then, he is a man of great experience ?"

" He is : has been in the trade thirty-five years, twenty of
which he has been located on Broadway ; now he has these
spacious warerooms, corner of East Fourth street and Broad‑
way. Thus, by avoiding the enormous rents of Broadway, he
is enabled to sell at least twenty-five per cent. less than his
competitors on that thoroughfare."

" As much as that?" said Jonathan, astonished.

" Yes ; such warerooms as Mr. Ham occupies, would, on
Broadway, command a rent of $30,000 per annum, while where
he now is, one door from Broadway, the rent does not exceed
one-fourth of that sum."

So speaking, we entered the building, and Jonathan was
soon lost in admiration of the elegance and beauty of the va‑
rious styles.

When Jonathan had completed his purchase, he was told—
with pardonable pride—that in 1840-44-52 and 54 Mr. Ham
took the first premium from the American Institute, for the
best Carriage, over several of the first manufacturers in the
country, and in 1854-5 was awarded a gold medal, as the first
premium, by the Commissioners of the World's Fair, in New
York. And Jonathan was also told, that the manufacturing
facilities of this establishment were not excelled by any other
in the country—giving constant employment to 400 to 500 first-
class mechanics—and that the manufacture of carriages far sur‑
pass, in high finish, good workmanship and fine quality of stock,
any Broadway establishment. He has orders from every quarter
of the world—from Cuba, Mexico, England, France, China, &c.

" By the way, we were talking of sewing-machines a few
minutes ago. Let us drop in here, No. 609 Broadway, the office
of the Howe Sewing Machine Company, and see if we cannot
catch a glimpse of Mr. Elias Howe, the original inventor of the
sewing-machine "

"Nothing would please me more," said Jonathan delightedly.

"At any rate," I went on, "if we have not the good fortune
to see him, we shall be enabled to see the original machine
made by him, and patented in 1846."

After examining the machine, which embraces all the principles embodied in the present sewing-machines, the only improvement being in form and simplicity, we were told the mechanical history of Mr. Elias Howe, who is now the president of this company, giving each branch of the manufacture his immediate supervision.

It appears that, nearly a quarter of a century ago, Mr. Elias Howe, a native of Massachusetts, first conceived the idea of making a mechanical seamstress. His history is remarkable, and in some respects, presents a happy contrast to that of other great inventors, whose genius only brought them trouble and penury through life.

When only twenty-two years of age, whilst working as a mechanic, he conceived the project of making a sewing-machine. This was about the year 1841, at which time he was married and had a little family around him, for whom he had to labor hard throughout the day. In after hours he labored in his humble abode, at Cambridgeport, contriving the various movements of the machine.

The patient endurance, the intelligence, and the perseverance of Mr. Howe were destined to overcome all difficulties in his way; and on the 10th of September, 1846, he obtained his first patent.

Singularly enough, Americans failed to see the advantages of this invention, so it was sent to England, where the patent right was sold for £200, equal to about $1,000. Beyond that Mr. Howe did not benefit himself in England. Nothing daunted, he returned to America. In 1853 he granted his first license for the making of his machines, and by degrees, was enabled to re-purchase the patents he had sold in the days of his adversity. In 1855 he was in possession of the whole of them, and now receives a royalty upon every sewing-machine manufactured in the United States, which produces an income of $100,000 a year.

"An immense sum," said Jonathan.

"Yes ; but incomparably trifling, to the benefit he has conferred upon the world at large, by the gift of his labor-saving machinery."

"You are right."

" When the Prince of Wales was in this country," I informed Jonathan, " there was none among his *suite* that admired so much, and paid such attention to American art as he."

Jonathan seemed somewhat surprised at this statement, as it was apparently apropos of nothing. Noticing this, I continued : " I was led to these remarks by our arriving at Gurney's Photographic and Fine Art Gallery, 707 Broadway. It is the oldest house in the country ; and it is here the Prince of Wales sat for his portrait "

" A photographic portrait ?' "

" Yes ; but afterwards finished in oil, by Mr. Constant Mayer, the well-known artist of the establishment. It was sent to Queen Victoria as a present, who was so pleased with it, that she sent a letter of thanks to the Messrs. Gurney, for the beautiful specimen of American art, and as an assurance of her appreciation of the skill with which it was executed."

" Quite a feather in their cap, I declare. "

" Accompanying the portrait was an album of photographs, which was presented to the Prince of Wales. He was so pleased with them, that he caused a splendid gold medal to be struck off, and sent to New York, for their acceptance."

" That shows most conclusively that American art is recognized abroad."

" Indeed it does. In the portrait gallery may be seen several fine specimens of the rare skill and power of these artists ; two are especially worthy of notice ; they are likenesses of the greatest generals of the day, Winfield Scott and U. S. Grant."

Jonathan, wishing to see these portraits, we entered the splendid art gallery of the Messrs. Gurney.

Before leaving, we were shown the latest novelty in the art, a microscopic photograph—a picture not larger than the eye of a needle—set with a lens which enlarges it to nearly life size. It is a pretty article of ornament, and enables the possessor to carry about with him, in the smallest space, and in the most unsuspected manner, a complete representation of the most precious of friends or lovers.

" The next hotel of any note on Broadway is the New York Hotel, extending from Washington to Waverly Place. It is much frequented by Southerners, and conducted on the European plan."

"What large building is that?" asked Jonathan, indicating the object of inquiry with the aid of his dexter finger.

"That is Alexander T. Stewart's retail dry goods store ; it stands on the corner of Tenth street, and is one of the greatest emporiums for articles connected with that business the world ever saw."

"Is the whole of that large building used for the transaction of Mr. Stewart's retail business?"

"Yes ; and large as it is, I warrant it is none too commodious for the proper assortment and care of goods, and the accommodation of customers."

"I wonder Mr. Stewart should allow such a line of carriages to stand before his store-doors. Are they for hire ? or, is there some public place of amusement in the neighborhood, and they are waiting for the audience to come out?"

I could not refrain from laughing at this interrogatory.

"Those carriages," I replied, "are in waiting for those ladies who are now inside the store shopping."

"What! the whole of them?"

"Yes ; and if you will look up Tenth street, you will see the line extends some distance up there."

"What an immense business he must do!"

"You are right ; he does. There is no house, either in this country or in Europe, that does so large a retail trade. But that is not to be wondered at, for no house has so large and varied an assortment. No matter what a purchaser requires— a pair of gloves, a silk dress, a lace shawl, or a parlor-carpet— she is sure to find a more varied and choice assortment of goods here than at any other house in the same line of business."

"Their trade is wholly with fashionable people, I presume?"

"The greater portion of their trade is with the *elite* of the city ; but people not so well to do in the world, also make their purchases here, finding it their interest to do so. For this reason, Mr. Stewart's facilities for buying are so large, and his purchases so great, that he is enabled to sell goods at a more reasonable rate than smaller houses."

"Ah! It is an old and true saying, that 'money makes money.'"

On the north-east corner of the same street is Grace church; one of the most fashionable places of worship in the city. It is Protestant Episcopal in its denomination, and the Rev. Dr. Thomas N. Taylor is the rector."

"It is a splendid edifice," ejaculated Jonathan, admiringly.

"It is; but some are of opinion it is too richly decorated for a religious edifice. There are upward of forty windows of stained glass, all of which have decided artistic merit, and well worthy inspection."

"The famous Diamond Wedding was celebrated here, if I am not mistaken?"

"You are right. The sexton of this church is the well-known Isaac V. Brown, without whom, as master of the ceremonies, no fashionable wedding is considered complete."

"My goodness!" ejaculated Jonathan Griggs, as we stopped on the corner of Eleventh street. "Is this another hotel? Why, New York seems full of them!"

"This is the St. Denis," I replied. "It is considered, architecturally, one of the handsomest buildings on Broadway. It is conducted on the European plan, and much frequented by foreigners."

Among the well-known art emporiums of Broadway, there is none better known than that of Messrs. Weisman & Langerfeldt, successors to Emil Seitz, the well-known *virtuoso*.

Mr. Seitz has been for years connected with fine art establishments, both in this country and in Europe, and has obtained one of the finest collections of line engravings, etchings, mezzotints, drawing studies, water-color drawings, &c., ever seen on this continent.

Now, on his retirement from business, he has transferred the whole of his business to the above-named gentlemen, who, from a long experience, are worthy to fill the place left vacant by the retirement of Mr. Seitz.

Their store is at No. 842 Broadway, corner of Thirteenth street, and will be found one of the centres of attraction on that far-famed street.

"What delightful place is this?" queried Jonathan, when we had reached Union Square.

"This," said I, "is Union Square, and extends from Four-teenth to Seventeenth streets. In the centre is a charming pleasure ground, surrounded by an iron railing. In it are a fountain, and a moderately large basin of water, filled with fish. It is a place of favorite resort during the summer months, and is much affected by nursemaids and their infantile cares."

"Such a spot in the heart of a great city, is like an oasis in the desert."

"Quite poetical, I declare," I laughingly replied. "On the northern side of the square are the Everett House, the Claren-don Hotel, and the headquarters of the Fenian Brotherhood ; on the western side are Dr. Cheever's church, famous for its Abo-lition proclivities, and the Spingler Hotel ; on the southern side are the Union Hotel, and the *Maison Doree*, celebrated as one of the best restaurants in the city."

"What statue is that?"

"That is the bronze statue of the immortal Washington. It was designed and executed by Mr. Brown, who was four years completing his task. It is fourteen and a half feet in height, and the extreme elevation, including the pedestal, which is of granite, is twenty-nine feet."

"What is the expense of such a statue?"

"This one cost upwards of $30,000. On the opposite side of the square, on the Fourteenth street side, a companion statue of Abraham Lincoln is to be erected."

Jonathan went nearer, to examine the statue, and as he did so, reverently raised his hat.

"Just round the corner," I remarked to Jonathan, "is the salesrooms of the largest piano-forte manufacturers in the whole wide world."

"How very singular," exclaimed Griggs. "I was just about to tell you that I had promised, while in New York, to purchase a piano for my daughter."

"Then Steinway's is the very place ; for they are not only the largest manufacturers in the world, but the best, as you

will readily believe, when I tell you they are endorsed by such
pianists and musical celebrities as S. B. Mills, Robert Gold-
beck, Theodore Thomas, Max Maretzek, Robert Heller, Carl
Bergmann, William Mason, and a host of others, equally well
known in the musical and operatic world."

" You don't say so!"

" And they are equally well known and sought after
throughout the whole of Europe. In London, at the Great
Exhibition of 1862, the Messrs. Steinway carried off the first
prize; indeed, so great was the superiority over all other
pianos, that the jury not only awarded a prize, but a high en-
comium upon the fortunate makers."

" Do you mean to say, the Steinway pianos are superior to
those made in Europe?"

" I do, indeed; but when I say so, I am only reiterating the
statement of the most celebrated Professors of Music throughout the whole of Europe."

" Are these the salesrooms?" asked Jonathan, as we stopped
before No's. 71 and 73 East Fourteenth street, between Union
Square and the Academy of Music. " Why, it is like a palace!"

" It is; and fully deserves that name. It is, as you see,
built of white marble, has a front on Fourteenth street of 50
feet, and a depth of 85 feet. It has a basement and four
stories, the whole of which are used as salesrooms for the sale
of their Square, Upright and Grand Pianos."

So saying, we entered the building, and Jonathan was at
once struck by the elegant and commodious salesrooms. After
Jonathan had made his purchase, I casually mentioned, he was
a stranger in the city, and was surprised at the magnificence and
extent of their building.

The salesman, with pardonable pride, admitted it to be a
splendid edifice, and informed us that a new Music Hall, to extend through to Fifteenth street, was being erected in the rear
of this building, which, when finished, would be 123 feet long,
75 feet in breadth, 42 feet high, and capable of holding 3,000
persons. He also told us that everything would be done to
make it the finest Music Hall in the country; between the
flooring and the ceiling of the basement will be a heavy coat-

STEINWAY & SONS' WAREROOMS, 71 & 73 E. 14th St.

ing of solid cement. This will prevent vibration, and add greatly to the acoustic properties of the hall. A new Grand Organ will also be erected, enabling music to be performed never before attempted in this country, such as Oratorios and Festivals. And, in case of fire, every precaution will be made, so that the audience will be enabled to effect an exit in a few seconds.

As we were about leaving the building, we were asked if we would not like to visit their Mammoth Piano-forte Manufactory.

To this question we gladly answered in the affirmative. So, being furnished with the necessary credentials, we at once proceeded, by cars, to this superb edifice, which is situated on Fourth avenue, occupying an entire block, extending from Fifty-second to Fifty-third streets.

Upon our arrival, we were received most courteously by one of the partners, who at once showed us round the building, and explained to us objects of interest.

"The front of this building, our manufactory," said he, "has a length of 201 feet, with a depth of 40 feet. The wings, on Fifty-second and Fifty-third streets, are each 165 feet in length, and 40 feet in depth. The whole building is six stories high, including the basement; the architecture is of the modern Italian style, with brick lintel arches, brown-stone trimmings, and brick dental cornices."

"It seems very substantially built," I remarked.

"It is; the basement wall is grouted brick, two feet thick; the first story walls twenty inches, and the upper walls sixteen inches in thickness. The main buildings cover fourteen city lots, twelve other lots are also used for the purpose of seasoning lumber, of which there is a stock of about 3,000,000 feet always piled up on the grounds."

"How long a time must elapse, before you consider your timber properly seasoned?" inquired Jonathan

"Two years. Not a piece of lumber is used in the manufacture of our pianos that has not been in the open air for that time, and subjected, also, to the kiln-drying process for a period of three months."

"The kiln-drying process?" interrogated Griggs.

" Yes. In the yard, here, as you perceive, there are four
drying houses, each of which is heated by 2,000 feet of steam
pipe, and contains about 75,000 feet of lumber ; consequently
there are about 300,000 feet of lumber constantly under the
process of kiln-drying. Here, also, is a splendid engine, of
fifty horse power, as well as three steam boilers of fifty horse
power each. In the basement of the Fifty-second street wing,
there is a supplementary engine, of twenty horse-power, so as
to guard against any accidental interruption."

" A most proper precaution."

"All the heavier portion of machinery is located in this
room," said our guide, as he led the way to the basement of
the Fifty-third street wing. "These planers, of which there
are three, were made expressly for our establishment, and are
the largest implements of their class existing, planing the largest
piano top or bottom at once. Here, also, are the up-and-down
saws, circular saws, and turning lathes. These wonderful and
powerful pieces of mechanism are constantly at work, shaping
the rough plank, ready for use on the first floor above, where
the bottoms, blockings, wrest-planks, and other parts of the
case, are gotten up, with the aid of moulding, joining, and
other machinery. On the third floor is located all the finer
machinery for scroll-sawing, rounding- corners, and shaping
the various parts of mechanism."

" Wonderful, most wonderful !" interrupted Jonathan.

" The floor above," continued our explanator, " and the corresponding floor, in the wing on Fifty-second street, are occupied by the casemakers, who take all these single parts, put
them together, veneer and finish, ready for the varnish-room,
on the top floor."

" The varnishing, I presume, does not take long."

" To varnish a case thoroughly takes three months."

" No : I never should have believed it."

" On the floor below, the instruments are strung, the action
and key-boards fitted in, and the tops, legs and lyres adjusted
and put on. The partly finished instruments are then taken
to the floor below, where the action is regulated · thence to

the first floor, where the hammers and the tone are regulated ; after which the final polish is put on the cases, and the perfect piano is ready to be sent to the salesroom.''

"How many workmen do you employ?'' asked Jonathan Griggs. "If it's a fair question?'' he added apologetically.

"We have about 450 men constantly employed, who turn out, on an average, 35 Square, 7 Grand, and 3 Upright Pianos—in all, 45 instruments a week. Nearly 800 pianos are constantly in course of construction ; and these, in connection with the hardware, machinery, engine, veneers, lumber, &c., &c., represent, at least, the sum of $450,000, exclusive of the buildings, the cost of which, and ground, were about $150,000. Of course, this does not include our building on Fourteenth street, which represents, at the present value of property, one million of dollars.''

"Goodness gracious ! It seems incredible.''

"It will not, when I tell you, that our annual sales are over a million and a quarter dollars, on which we have to pay a revenue tax of over $75,000.''

"So large a business must be systematized to a nicety,'' spoke Jonathan.

"Our business is divided into eighteen different departments, each under the immediate superintendence of a skilful foreman, who is responsible for the work done in his special department.''

"And quite right, too.''

"No person is allowed to change from one branch to another, each workman having but one department of labor, by constant application to which much greater skill is acquired than can be attained in smaller factories, where the several different branches are performed by the same person.''

"An excellent plan, truly.''

"We never employ apprentices—only the most skilled artizans. Indeed, our standard of excellence is so high, that it is a frequent occurrence for a workman who has long given satisfaction in other factories, to fail in achieving it with us.''

"And these foremen, of whom you have spoken, I presume are overlooked by members of the firm.''

" Yes, our firm consists of father and three sons, who have under their immediate personal supervision, the construction of every instrument, from the selection of the rough lumber until the finished piano is sent to the salesrooms."

Thanking our guide for his kindness and courtesy, we withdrew, and once more returned to Union Square, and resumed our walk on Broadway.

Jonathan, by this time, was becoming tired, so we sauntered leisurely further up Broadway, taking a casual glance at Moore's Madison Square Hotel, corner of Twenty-first street, and the St. Germaine, occupying the block on Twenty-second street, between Broadway and Fifth avenue.

" At No. 940 Broadway," said I to Jonathan, " the corner of Twenty-second street, is the new store of N. Grossmayer, who has lately opened a large and fine clothing establishment. The proprietor keeps constantly on hand a large and varied assortment of goods, both ready made and to measure. The cutters are the best that can be obtained, while for elegance of style, workmanship and durability of material, Mr. Grossmayer's goods cannot be excelled by any other house in the trade."

"This hotel," I said, pointing to the white marble building, occupying the block between Twenty-third and Twenty-fourth streets, " is the celebrated Fifth Avenue Hotel, and is one of the largest in the city, having accommodations for nearly eight hundred guests."

" You surprise me."

" Let me draw your attention to the magnificent drug store under the hotel, and at the corner of Twenty-fourth street."

" It is, indeed, a superb place."

"The proprietors are Messrs. Casewell, Mack & Co., and their store is generally acknowledged, both by foreigners and travelled residents, to be the finest and most spacious establishment of the kind in the world. It is well worthy a view, and all strangers should certainly pay a visit to it before leaving the city. From that marble tank, which you see, is drawn the celebrated spring waters of Europe, such as Kissengen, Vichy, Pyrmont, &c., all kept at the same temperature as

STEINWAY & SONS' PIANO MANUFACTORY, 4th Ave. & 52d Street.

that obtained immediately at the springs. Another feature of this truly magnificent establishment, is the deliciously cool soda water, with the choicest fruit syrups, passed through a mass of Rockland Lake ice, and drawn from the grand fountain you see near the entrance."

"How my mouth waters for it!" exclaimed Jonathan.

"This house also manufactures that best of all tonics, the Ferro-phosphorated Elixir of Calisaya Bark, which you meet from Canada to New Orleans, and even to San Francisco: besides, they make Hazard & Caswell's Cod-Liver Oil, which has, among the medical profession generally, the reputation of being the purest and sweetest in the world: they also manufacture the famous Toilet Cologne, ' No. 6,' now famous all over the country. Every article emanating from their establishment, is of the choicest quality. With the fashionable, this establishment is a great favorite, as is their branch house, at Newport, R. I."

"What park is that?"

"That is Madison Square, and contains about 10 acres of land; in it are many noble trees, and in summer, the grass and shrubs are pleasant to the eyes of many weary New Yorkers, who come here to relieve themselves of the dull monotony of so much bricks and mortar."

"What is that tall, pillar-like looking thing, sticking up there?"

" That is a granite shaft, erected by the Common Council of the city of New York, to General Worth, who fell during the Mexican war. If you are asked, you can say it is situated on the western side of Madison Square."

As Jonathan was examining the monument, a carriage drove rapidly up to the Hoffman House, which is exactly opposite, and situated on the corner of Twenty-fifth street, at the junction of Fifth avenue and Broadway, and a small crowd almost instantaneously collected."

"We are fortunate," I cried; "General Scott must be in that carriage."

"What! General Winfield Scott, the old Mexican hero?"

And Jonathan, with an agility worthy of a much younger

man, darted into the crowd, eager to catch a glimpse of the veteran, for it was he, indeed. In another instant, the tall, commanding figure of the General descended from the carriage, and, amid a few cheers, which he acknowledged, entered the hotel.

"The sight of General Scott is, alone, worth a visit to New York," said Jonathan, decidedly, and then added, "I wonder what he is going to do inside."

"He lives at the Hoffman House, and has done so since it was first opened, in 1864."

"You don't tell me! It is a splendid-looking house, and, looking upon Mad'son Square, as it does, and being on Fifth avenue, at the junction of Broadway, through which a constant stream of gay and dashing equipages are constantly passing to and from the Central Park, must make it additionally pleasant to those stopping there."

"It does. This house is the representative house of its kind in New York, and is conducted on the European plan. It has accommodations for nearly 400 guests; yet, great as this number is, it is invariably filled with the *elite* and fashion of the country."

"Who are the proprietors?"

"Messrs. Mitchell and Read, gentlemen whose names, to the hotel-going public, are a sufficient guarantee for the excellence of their house, and the superiority of their accommodations."

"John," said Jonathan, interrupting me, with an air of profound wisdom, "I am getting very tired."

"Are you?" I replied, assuming a dubious tone. To tell the truth, I was tired myself, but I would not have owned it for the world.

"Yes; let us be getting home."

So we returned to my house. Jonathan was so completely worn out, that he actually fell asleep over his supper, which, I observing, suggested a bed as the better place to slumber in.

Bidding me good night, he retired to his room. I soon followed his example, and was quickly off to the land of dreams.

WALK THE SECOND.

CENTRAL PARK.

It was a beautiful morning. As I drew up the window-shade and threw open the blinds, the sun streamed in brightly through my chamber window, lighting up my room and infusing a cheeriness in me perfectly delightful.

"Just the day for my purpose," I thought. "Nature will appear in her most delightful garb, and if I don't astonish Jonathan, I'm a Dutchman."

So, dressing with rather more than my usual care—for I hold that, when visiting a beautiful place, you should not help to mar the general whole by being badly dressed—I proceeded to the breakfast-room, there to wait for Jonathan, in order to partake of the matutinal meal.

I read all the morning papers, wrote a couple of letters, drummed one or two tunes with my fingers on the window-panes, and still no Jonathan appeared. Becoming impatient, I rang the bell, and asked Mary if she had called Mr. Griggs.

"Oh! yes, sir," she replied; "I called him when I called you."

"Strange he does not appear. He must take a very long while dressing. Mary, just run up stairs, will you, and tell Mr. Griggs breakfast is ready."

Mary departed on her errand; quickly returned with the information that Mr. Griggs would be down directly. He was as good as his word, for almost before Mary had left the room, he bustled in.

"How now, laggard?" I said. "Breakfast has been ready this hour."

"No! Has it, though? I am very sorry to have kept you waiting, but the fact is, I overslept myself."

"Your walk yesterday was too much for you," I said, laughing.

"Well, to tell you the truth, John, I was very tired. I think walking on pavement is more fatiguing than walking on soil; don't you?"

"No doubt,' I replied, somewhat drily, "to those not accustomed to pavement, it must be tiresome."

"Ah! that accounts for it, then; for I think I never was so tired in all my life before, and never rose from my bed so reluctantly"

I was not sorry to hear this. I, also, was excessively tired, but, of course, did not own it, and began to think my prowess as a pedestrian was on the wane. Jonathan's confession, however, reassured me, as he was the very picture of robust health and strength.

"To-day, Jonathan," I said, "we will have a rest."

"What! not go out to-day?" and Griggs' face assumed an expression of blank dismay. "I haven't tired you out?"

"Tired me out!" and I laughed heartily at the idea. "No, no, Jonathan; you nor no other man can do that. But what I meant was to-day we'll take a carriage."

"A carriage!"

"You may well look surprised. To-day, a carriage is an imperative necessity. What I am going to show you to-day would take two or three weeks to explore properly on foot."

"Nonsense!"

"No nonsense at all about it. Could you examine in one day, and on foot, nearly forty miles of walks, rides, and drives?"

I would here mention that there are only about thirty-eight miles, but when talking to a friend, it is as well to give the round number and say forty.

"I don't think I could; in fact, I am sure I could not. But what wonderful place is this you intend taking me to?"

"Not more than eight years ago," I continued, not heeding him, "it was a bleak and barren spot, with scarcely the slightest vestige of vegetation; the accumulated filth of bone-boiling establishments and other offensive refuse matter was gathered there; stagnant pools of slimy mud and water infected the air with malarious diseases; dead dogs and cats were strewn about in reckless profusion, poisoning the atmosphere and offending the olfactories of those who were luckless enough to pass that way."

" You don't mean to take me there, do you ? " asked Jonathan, giving a little shudder.

" Now," I went on to say, paying no attention to his question, " it is one of the most beautiful and charming places on the face of the earth. The whole scene has been changed as if by enchantment. Instead of stagnant pools of water, are a beautiful lake, waterfalls, and pure crystal streams. Instead, of dead and putrid animals, the air is redolent with the perfume of a thousand flowers ; and instead of a bleak, barren spot, the whole is alive with vegetation."

" What place is this ? "

" Can you not guess ? "

" I think I can," said Jonathan, as eagerly as though I had propounded a conundrum ; " you mean the Central Park."

" I do. What other could I mean ! For there is none like it—none."

" I have read so much about it that I am anxious to see it. When do we start ? "

" At once, if you have finished breakfast. I heard the carriage arrive some few minutes ago."

" Then let us be off ; " and Jonathan put on his hat and pulled on his gloves in the most expeditious manner imaginable.

" If," said I, as we were being rapidly whirled toward the Park, " on your return home, you wish to post any of your Western friends who intend visiting New York on the best way of reaching the Park, you—"

" One moment, if you please ; " and in less than that time he was ready with note-book and pencil to jot down what information I might give.

" You must tell them," I went on, " that the cars of the Third or Sixth Avenue Railroads will take them there. The latter will deposit them at one of the principal gates ; the former, within a short distance. If they wish to hire a carriage, as we have done, let them hire one from some respect-

ble livery stable, and not at the entrance of the Park gates.
If they do, the driver may not demand an exorbitant fare;
but if he does, the Park Commissioners are not to blame, as
they are entirely beyond their control."

Jonathan spoke not a word, but went on busily writing.

"During the months of December, January, and February,
the gates are open from 7 A.M. to 8 P.M.; during March, April,
May, June, October, and November, from 6 A.M. to 9 P.M.;
during July, August, and September, from 5 A.M. to 11 P.M."

"At what period of the year do you think it best to visit
the Park?"

"That is impossible to say, as Nature at all seasons of the
year has its peculiar charms, and at all times, providing the
weather is not too inclement, the Central Park is a delightful
place to visit."

"How large is the Park?" asked Jonathan.

"The length, from 59th to 110th Streets, is 13,507 ft.
9 4-10 in.; breadth, from 5th to 8th Avenues, 2,718 ft.
6 9-10 in.; making a superficial area of 843 019-1000 acres."

"I could never have remembered all that," said Jonathan.

"Neither could I, if I had not read up just before I left
home. But here we are at the Park," I said, as the carriage
rolled slowly in at the Scholar's Gate, corner of 5th Avenue
and 59th Street.

"The Scholar's Gate!" exclaimed Griggs; "is that the gate
for scholars to go through?"

"Yes, or for any one else who likes. There are sixteen gates,
all of which are named. Besides the Scholar's Gate, there are
the Artist's Gate, situated on 6th Avenue and 59th Street;
the Artizan's Gate, 7th Avenue and 59th Street; the Merchant's Gate, 8th Avenue and 59th Street; the Women's Gate,
8th Avenue and 72d Street; the Hunter's Gate, 8th Avenue
and 79th Street; the Mariner's Gate, 8th Avenue and 85th
Street; the Gate of All Saints, 8th Avenue and 96th Street;
the Boy's Gate, 8th Avenue and 100th Street; the Children's
Gate, 5th Avenue and 72d Street; the Engineer's and Miner's
Gate, 5th Avenue and 79th Street; the Stranger's Gate, 5th
Avenue and 90th Street; the Woodman's Gate, 5th Avenue

and 96th Street ; the Girl's Gate, 5th Avenue and 102d Street ; the Farmer's Gate, 6th Avenue and 110th Street ; the Warrior's Gate, 7th Avenue and 110th Street."

Telling the coachman to stop at the entrance of the Mall, we alighted, as I wished Jonathan to view the terrace and fountain, which he could not do in a carriage.

" This noble avenue," I commenced, "lined on either side with trees, and called the Mall, is 1,112 feet long and 35 feet in width. On the right, as you enter," said I, pointing to the spot, "is the site of the Shakespeare Monument. At the end of the Mall is the Water Terrace, from which we can obtain an excellent view of the lake."

" What are those birds?" asked Griggs, pointing to the waterfowl floating calmly on the bosom of the lake.

" Those are swans, presented to the Commissioners by the Senate of the City of Hamburg ; by the Worshipful Company of Vintners, London ; and by the Worshipful Company of Dyers, London."

" And there are row-boats, too, upon the lake ! "

" Yes, and for viewing the beauties of the lake no better means could be obtained, as our citizens are fully aware, for the revenue derived from them is between six and seven thousand dollars yearly."

" What is that strange-looking craft ? "

" That is a Venetian gondola. If you wish to imagine yourself in the ' land of romance, poetry, and song,' all you have to do is to hire that, and give your fancy full play ; but be careful not to speak to the gondolier, for he might answer you with an Hibernian accent, and dispel the illusion."

Jonathan laughed.

" This terrace, upon which we now stand, is the main architectural structure of the Park. It is the principal assembling place for pedestrians, and an expenditure has been made upon it commensurate with the important position it holds."

" It is certainly very beautiful," said Jonathan, looking round admiringly.

" In the elaboration of details and purity of execution, the architect has elicited universal admiration. On the Esplanade, just beneath us, is a most beautiful fountain, the chief figure of which is Peace, bearing the olive branch, designed and modeled by Miss Emma Stebbins."

"It is like fairy-land!" was all that Jonathan said, giving a sigh of pleasure.

"On the left of the Mall, near the Terrace, is the Music Hall. Every Saturday afternoon during the summer, weather permitting, mus'cal entertainments are given. On such occasions the Park is crowded ; indeed, so much so, that the Commissioners are at a loss how to provide seats, or even standing room within convenient distances for hearing, and have in contemplation the establishment of another band at some other locality of the park."

"Music hath charms, indeed," said Jonathan.

"The programmes are varied, and interspersed with national airs from the music of other countries, that the stranger who may be present, catching the sound of a familiar air, may feel that in this city he finds a welcome."

"Nothing left undone that can contribute to the comfort and happiness of anybody. Look, look at that little bird perched on the rim of that basin, and drinking."

"It is a sparrow. Fourteen of them were brought from Europe, in 1863 ; they were let loose in the park, and have largely increased in numbers. They are very tame, and are much valued for their capacity for consuming worms and insects."

Having previously told the driver of the carriage to meet us on the drive, west of the terrace, there was no occasion for us to retrace our steps ; so, once more getting in, I told him to carry us to the grand Croton Reservoir.

"This," said I, as soon as we arrived at the reservoir, "is York Hill."

"What a body of water!" exclaimed Jonathan.

"It is immense ; but not too large for the requirements of New Yorkers. The water surface is about ninety-six acres ; the depth of water, when full, about thirty-eight feet, and its capacity more than a billion of New York gallons."

"You surprise me."

" The gate-houses," I continued, " one of which is on the north, the other on the south side, cost nearly two hundred thousand dollars, and the masonry of the reservoir nearly six hundred thousand dollars."

" Almost incredible!" was all that Jonathan could say.

" Two miles from here, on Murray Hill, is the distributing reservoir, its capacity being a hundred and fifty millions of gallons. It is built in the Egyptian style of architecture, and cost nearly fourteen millions of dollars in building. On the walls is a promenade, much frequented by New Yorkers."

" What a number of fish !" ejaculated Jonathan. " Do they allow any one to angle here ?"

"Oh, no. The fish are guarded very carefully, as they are found to be very useful in devouring the animalculi, thus keeping the water pure."

Leaving the reservoir, we proceeded to the hill situated on the south side, from which an excellent view can be obtained of the whole Park.

" This walk," said I to Jonathan, " upon which we are now standing, is tunneled for a transverse road, four of which roads cross the Park, at the following places, viz. : at Sixty-fifth, Seventy-ninth, Eighty-fifth, and Ninety-seventh streets."

" What are the objects of these roads ?"

" When the Park was first contemplated, it was at once seen that to cause business vehicles, that wished to go from either side to the centre of the other, make the whole circuit of the Park, would be a waste of time, and a great obstruction to business. To allow them to go through the Park itself would never do : if they were allowed to, they would be extremely detrimental to the pleasure-seekers in their walks, rides and drives. So these four roads were constructed, and are found to answer, excellently well, the purposes for which they were intended."

" The trees are very young," said Jonathan, in a tone of voice that was meant to be disparaging

" They are," I replied ; but every year will help to rectify that. You must remember that I told you, only eight years ago the ground on which the Park is now situated, was a bleak and barren spot, almost destitute of vegetation."

" True ; so you did."

" Experience has shown," I went on, " that it is not, as a general rule, economical to plant trees of a very large size ; those of less size, carefully transplanted, and well cared for, being much less likely to fail in the process, and generally making far better trees."

"That's true."

" There are frequent instances of the successful transplantation of quite large trees, but the increased expense, and the great liability to die out, in from one to four years after their removal, point to the economy in time and money, in the ultimate perfectness of the trees, to the superiority of the practice of removing trees of the usual nursery sizes.

" I have found that out, in my orchard at home."

" In the first years of the Park there was great impatience expressed by the public for the immediate planting of large trees ; but with the growth of the earlier planted trees, this desire has yielded to a recognition of the necessity of time to produce trees of luxuriance of growth, and perfection of form."

" Is the whole of the Park inclosed by a wall like that?" asked Jonathan, pointing to it.

" Not yet; but it is rapidly being pushed forward toward completion. When finished, exclusive of gateways, and of such portions as will, at present, from the precipitousness of the rock, require no enclosure, the total length of the wall will be 29,025 feet, or about seven miles."

Once more accepting the help of the carriage, we were driven to the Great Hill, situated on the north-west corner of the Park.

" Here," said I, " on the brow of these broken and precipitous hills, may still be seen the remains of military fortifications, consisting of breastworks of earth, about three feet in height."

" When do you think these breastworks were erected?" inquired Jonathan, deeply interested.

"They, no doubt, formed a part of a chain of fortifications of the war of 1812, that extended from the Harlem to the Hudson river, passing across the Park, to a point a little west of what is now the Eighth avenue, and extending along the rocky eminence on the west of the plains, to Manhattanville. The stone structure, still standing on this rocky bluff, formed a portion of the line.''

'' How very interesting !''

'' On the northern side of this hill, about two feet below the surface, the remains of a military encampment were found. The ground, in spaces of about eight feet square, was compactly trodden, and in a corner of each space was a recess, rudely built of stone, for a fire-place, with straps of iron, that seemed to have been used in cooking. Shot and bayonets were also found in the vicinity.''

'' And were these some of the relics of 1812, too ?''

'' There is sufficient known of the history of this property, to warrant the belief, that it was passed over, and perhaps occupied during the year 1776, by the British and Hessian troops, shortly after their landing on the island, and that it was occupied in the war of 1812 by the American soldiers.''

'' Quite historical ground, I declare.''

'' The relics alluded to, in all probability, belonged to the latter period. It is the intention of the Commissioners to preserve, as far as practicable, the remains of these works, that so much enhance the interest of this section of the Park.''

'' And very right, too, for every year will add to their interest.''

'' Let us retrace our steps,'' I said, '' and pay a visit to the menagerie ''

'' Is there a collection of animals here ?'' asked Jonathan, surprised.

'' Oh, yes ; it is situated on the eastern side of the Mall. The collection, though not large, is excessively interesting, and well worth looking at. It is increasing, however, very rapidly, by gifts from those interested in the subject, both at home and abroad.''

After looking at the animals, we proceeded to the west side of the Mall ; there I showed Jonathan the oak and elm trees that were planted by the Prince of Wales, on his visit to this country, in 1860.

Thence we went to the play-ground, situated at the south-west portion of the Park, which is used by our citizens, both children and adults, as a cricket and base-ball ground. It is the object of the Commissioners of the Park, to encourage the more organized and active exercises, sports and amusements ; to this end, the ground is well kept and cared for by the keepers, and every facility and protection is given to the players.

During the past year, nearly seven millions of persons visited the Park, and out of that immense number, only a few over a hundred were arrested, and those for minor transgressions, committed generally through thoughtlessness, and a want of familiarity with the rules of the Park. Thus showing a general disposition prevailing among those who resort to the Park, to conform to the prescribed regulations.

The number of equestrians and vehicles entering the Park, is the largest between 4 and 5 P.M. During three months of the year, viz. : June, July and August, the greatest number enter at a later hour.

Yearly the attractions of this pleasant ground are increasing. The foliage becoming dense with the lapse of time, constantly presents new and more striking effects. The planting has been done, in areas as the ground was prepared ; upon some portions, consequently, the growth gives evidence of more maturity than upon others. Already, in some parts of the Park, there is sufficient development to readily lead the imagination to realize, in some measure, beauties which the hand of nature will perfect in her own good time.

It is from the fields and the flowers, the festooning of the climbing vine, the many-shaped and many-colored drapery of the forest, and from the green carpeting of the lawn, that the most refined gratifications are derived. These, to the lover of nature, are always sources of pure enjoyment, and, in their perfect development, afford pleasure to vast numbers, in modes to which it will be difficult to take exception.

If other countries excel in the magnitude of the products of the animal kingdom, by general assent, naturalists accord to our own continent marked superiority of vegetable life. Its trees are peculiarly numerous and majestic, its fields luxuriant and prolific, its flowers brilliant and varied. So far as is consistent with the convenient use of the grounds, vegetation holds the first place of distinction ; it is the work of nature, invulnerable to criticism, accepted by all, as well by the ignorant as the cultivated, and affords a limitless field for interesting observation and instruction.

Thus did I hold forth to Griggs, as we were whirled rapidly homeward. Turning to ask him if he did not agree with me, I found he was fast asleep.

"Jonathan," I cried, shaking him, "wake up. Here have I been talking to you for the last twenty minutes, and I might just as well have talked to the wind."

"Excuse me, John ; but the fact is, I'm very tired, and fell asleep before I was aware of it. Pray go on with what you were saying."

"I was about to tell you, Jonathan, of the appearance of the Park in winter, but as you are tired, I will defer it till some future time."

"I beg of you not to ; do go on ; I promise not to become somnolent again."

"During the winter," I commenced, "when the condition of the lake will permit, skating is the favorite pastime of those who visit the Park. Often twenty or thirty thousand people enjoying this healthy recreation at the same time."

Jonathan here made a sort of guttural sound, that I thought was one of approval.

"Ladies, too, are great skaters. There is not a prettier sight in the wide world than seeing a young and pretty girl upon skates. The grace she exhibits is bewildering ; many a young fellow has lost his heart, and skated himself into matrimony, on the Central Park pond."

At this juncture, the carriage stopped at my door. Alighting, I look round for Jonathan ; finding he did not follow, I returned to see the cause, and discovered he was fast asleep again.

"The Central Park," said Jonathan, when I had aroused him, "is a very beautiful place, but it is somewhat tiring to endeavor to view it all in one day."

So saying, he retired to his own room, and I did not see him for several hours.

WALK THE THIRD.

PUBLIC AND BENEVOLENT INSTITUTIONS.

This, the third day of Jonathan's visit, we were up by times, and started at an early hour on our tour of inspection. My friend Griggs was anxious to see the Halls of Justice, or, as they are more familiarly termed, on account of their gloomy and doleful aspect, "The Tombs."

"The Tombs" is a large and spacious building, or rather, series of buildings, situated on Centre street, occupying the whole block, and running through to Elm street, both on the Franklin and Leonard streets sides. It is built in the Egyptian style, and the melancholy aspect of the building makes one give an involuntary shiver as he passes.

Having obtained the necessary permit, procurable at No. 1 Bond street, we presented it to Mr. James E. Coulter, the warden, who at once proceeded to show us the prison.

From him we learned that there are three other city prisons, besides "The Tombs," viz.: Essex Market, Jefferson Market, and Fifty-seventh street prison. All prisoners committed for trial by the criminal courts are sent to the "Tombs" for safe keeping. During the past year, the total number of prisoners committed to the city prisons was thirty-nine thousand six hundred and sixteen, being an increase over the previous year, of eight thousand three hundred and eighty-three.

Leading the way to the male department of the prison, on the first tier of which are the cells, eleven in number, where prisoners condemned to the State Prison, or under sentence of death, are confined. Also, on this tier, are six more cells for the accommodation of prisoners convicted of minor offences; likewise six cells used for hospital purposes. On the second and third tiers are sixty more cells, for prisoners charged with felony—making, in all, eighty-five cells in the male department.

For the confinement of female prisoners, there are twenty-two cells ; eleven of which are used for those accused of grave offences, the remainder for women committed for intoxication and disorderly conduct.

Thus it will be seen, there are one hundred and seven cells in the "Tombs," but this number is found inadequate to the proper care and reception of all the prisoners confined therein. Many have to be confined in the same cell, and the evils arising from so doing cannot-be over-estimated. So, it is in contemplation to enlarge the present, or build a new prison.

The average cost of keeping a prisoner in food, clothing and bedding, is a fraction over thirty cents per day.

We were also shown the court-yard, in which criminals suffer the extreme penalty of the law. Jonathan looked, with a strange fascination, upon the material used in the construction of the gallows, and gazed, with a sort of inquisitive awe, upon all the paraphernalia appertaining thereto.

Jonathan, contrary to his usual custom, had hardly spoken a word, and when we were once more fairly in the street, he gave a little sigh of relief, as if pleased at being once again outside of four such sombre-looking walls.

Our next visit was to the Custom House, through which the majority of the imports and exports of the country pass. It is located on Wall street, on the corner of William, and extends through to Exchange Place. It was formerly known as the Merchants' Exchange, and cost in building, including the ground on which it stands, nearly two millions of dollars. To the original stockholders it was not a successful undertaking— they losing every cent they had invested—a mortgage was upon it, and that was foreclosed by the Messrs. Barings, of London. Some few years ago it was purchased by the Government for the purpose which it is now used. The rotunda is well worthy of inspection, and gives at once a correct impression of the vastness of the interior of this building : it is capable of containing three thousand persons. It is built of blue Quincy granite ; is 200 feet in length, 171 feet in width, and the extreme elevation 124 feet.

I am not sure, but I am inclined to think, Jonathan was un-

der the impression he would see bulls and bears, and lame
ducks on Wall street, for he peered abont most curiously, and
finally asked me where those animals could be seen.

Laughingly, I explained the terms to him He looked somewhat sheepish, and told me he had only asked me for a joke—
he knew all the while they were men.

I pretended to believe him ; but I still have my doubts.

The splendid building of white marble, constructed in the
Doric order of architecture, at the corner of Wall and Nassau
streets, is the United States Sub Treasury and Assay Office.
It is 200 feet long, 80 feet wide, and 80 feet high. At the entrances on Wall and Pine streets, are handsome porticos, with
eight columns, purely Grecian. Each column is 5 feet 8
inches in diameter, and 32 feet high. Formerly it was occupied
as the Custom House, but not being large enough for the proper
transaction of its business, it was removed, as has just been
mentioned, to the old Merchants' Exchange.

Leaving Wall street, we passed up Nassau street, and, stopping opposite the Post Office, between Cedar and Liberty
streets, I pointed out the little wooden steeple, on the top of the
building, I said :

" In that steeple Benjamin Franklin many a time has prac-
tised his experiments in electricity."

"How very interesting !" Jonathan's note-book was out in
an instant, and he jotted down the historical fact.

" It was formerly the Middle Dutch Church, and when this
city was occupied by the British, was put to military uses by
them, and received much damage. Afterwards it was repaired,
and used for divine worship ; subsequently it was purchased by
the Government, and put to its present uses."

" It is not so large a building as I expected to see for a post
office in the Empire City."

"No; such an edifice is a disgrace to the principal city of
the Western World. Everything is done, that space will permit, to facilitate the transaction of business, but the means
are totally inadequate, and how the clerks manage to get
through their multifarious duties, so cramped for room, is a
mystery."

"Why don't the Government build a new one?"

"It has been talked of for the last ten or twelve years; but nothing definite has been done. Some thought the present good enough; others wanted it removed further up town, while many thought if it were removed a step from its present site, the commercial interests of the city would be at stake."

"I should have thought they would have been enabled to have settled the matter in ten or twelve years."

"One would think so. But the Government are, apparently, acquainted with the fable of the old man and his ass, and know that striving to please everybody, you will please nobody, so have done nothing."

"If I had a. say in the matter," said Jonathan, "I would quickly have one built; for, in a city noted for such magnificent stores and public buildings, it is a shame for the Government to have such a mean and ugly-looking structure for a post office, which I presume is visited more by strangers than any other building in the city."

"You are right. If you, as a stranger, notice it, what an eyesore it must be to those who are resident, and have to visit it daily."

Jonathan wished to purchase some postage stamps, and was crossing the street for that purpose, when I stopped him, with the information, that time was money. And, if he had any regard for that axiom, it would be better for him to procure them at one of the stations up town.

"Here, in Nassau street, and vicinity, are the various newspaper offices, which I intend showing you—but not to-day. An especial pilgrimage must be paid to them."

"Whatever you say, John, I am entirely in your hands, and during my stay, you are my counsellor and guide.

On the corner of Elm and White streets is the lower City Arsenal; it is very strongly built, and is so constructed, that a company, of not more than fifty men, could protect it from the assault of any number. The upper floors are used as drill-rooms for a portion of the New York State Militia; the lower floor contains the artillery of the First Division. This and the new arsenal, at the junction of Thirty-fifth street and Seventh avenue, are connected by telegraph, so that in case of a riot uninterrupted communications could be had between the two buildings.

"Now," said I to Jonathan, "we will pay a visit to the 'Five Points.'"

"The 'Five Points!' I have heard of that before ; are you going alone?"

"Going alone! No ; I want you to accompany me."

"Yes, yes, of course. But I mean are you not going to obtain the company of a policeman for our protection?"

"Dear me, no. 'Five Points' is not what it used to be in your day. Now a person can visit there without fear of molestation ; fights and broils are the exception—not the rule. Not that I mean to say it is the quietest and most peaceable portion of New York, but it is a little elysium, compared to what it was some fifteen or twenty years ago."

"What has wrought this change?"

"That building!" and I pointed to the House of Industry, near Centre and Pearl streets.

"But how?"

"Listen, and I will tell you. In the year 1851, the Rev. L. M. Pease first established this institution. It was brought about by his witnessing the suffering of children, and the crime engendered by their being allowed to wander about the streets. So, with the assistance of a number of gentlemen, he established the House of Industry, and with the most beneficial results. Children are taught to read and write, and if, by diligence and good conduct, they are found sufficiently worthy, homes and situations are found for them out West, or in the country ; anywhere, in fact, out of the city, so as to wean them from old associates. Thus, an honest start in life is given them, and it is their own fault if they do not make good and respected members of society."

"A most philanthrophic and excellent plan."

"It," I continued, "is a receptacle for all who have nowhere else to go. The orphan, the deserted, the children of parents separated by convictions for crime, the offspring of those totally unable to support their children—all here find a home until they can be properly placed and cared for. They are cleansed, clothed, fed, taught, and furnished with labor as early as practicable.''

" Are men and women also assisted ?''

" Yes ; so far as it can be done, without encouraging a de pendence upon charity, and efforts are made to reform and procure labor for such as are willing to work. Since its foundation, nearly a thousand women have been sent to situations in different parts of the country. In short, this institution stands between wretchedness and crime, with open gates for all ''

Jumping into a Fourth avenue car, we rode to Astor Place ; thence walked to Lafayette Place, on which is situated the farfamed Astor Library. It is a grand edifice, built in the Romanesque style, and is constructed of brick, ornamented with brown stone. But the crowning glory is the interior, not in point of architecture—though that is beautiful enough—but in the long lines of stately and goodly books that that are ranged on shelves in the different alcoves of the building.

In this library there are already over one hundred thousand volumes, and additions are constantly being made by the learned librarian. Here may be seen the pale student, poring over some well-worn tome, that to the scholar is worth its weight in gold ; or, the man of leisure, who has just dropped in to wile away an hour ; or, the young lady who wishes to re-peruse once more her favorite novel. All, all are represented ; but quietness reigns supreme, and each man, as he enters, doffs his hat, out of respect to the dead and living authors that surround him.

It is free to all, and will stand as an everlasting monument to its founder, John Jacob Astor, who endowed it with the sum of $400,000.

At the junction of Third and Fourth avenues, occupying the entire block on both sides, and extending through to Eighth street, stands the Cooper Union, or, as it is more generally called, The Cooper Institute. It was built by Mr. Peter Cooper, at the cost of $300,000, and is devoted to the " moral, intellectual and physical improvement of his countrymen.'

In it are a free reading-room, supplied with foreign and do

mestic newspapers and magazines, a gallery of paintings and sculpture, and a school of design. The basement is fitted up as a lecture-room—the largest in the city—used chiefly for political meetings, but occasionally for lectures, concerts, and other entertainments of a kindred character.

The whole is under the control of a Board of Directors, who let out the first and second stories, which are arranged for stores and offices, so as to meet the current expenses of the In-titute. From this source an annual revenue of nearly $30,000 is obtained.

The American Institute is in this building, the object of which society is to promote and encourage new inventions in science and art. The annual fairs for that purpose are held under the auspices of this association. It has also a library, relating principally to the inventive and mechanical arts, and which, as books of reference, to inventors are invaluable.

On Astor Place, running through to Eighth street, is the Mercantile Library. The building is now called Clinton Hall, but was formerly the Astor Place Opera House, the scene of the notorious Macready riots. The library contains nearly 50,000 volumes, embracing nearly every department of knowl-edge. In the reading-room can be found nearly every periodi-cal published either in this country or Europe. It is, as the name indicates, expressly for the use of those engaged in mer-cantile pursuits—either merchants or their clerks. The former have to pay an annual subscription of $5; the latter, an ini-tiation fee of $1, and $2 subscription.

On the east side of Washington Square, formerly the site of a Potter's field, but now beautifully decorated with superb trees, shrubs, grass plats, gravel walks, and a fountain, is the New York University. The various departments of learning are governed by a chancellor, and a number of professors. Its reputation as a seat of learning stands high, and graduates are celebrated as scholars. It is built in the Gothic style of archi-tecture, and was erected in 1831. At the usual hours on Sun-days, divine service is held in the chapel.

On Eighth street, extending through to Ninth street, bounded by the Third and Fourth avenues, and occupying three

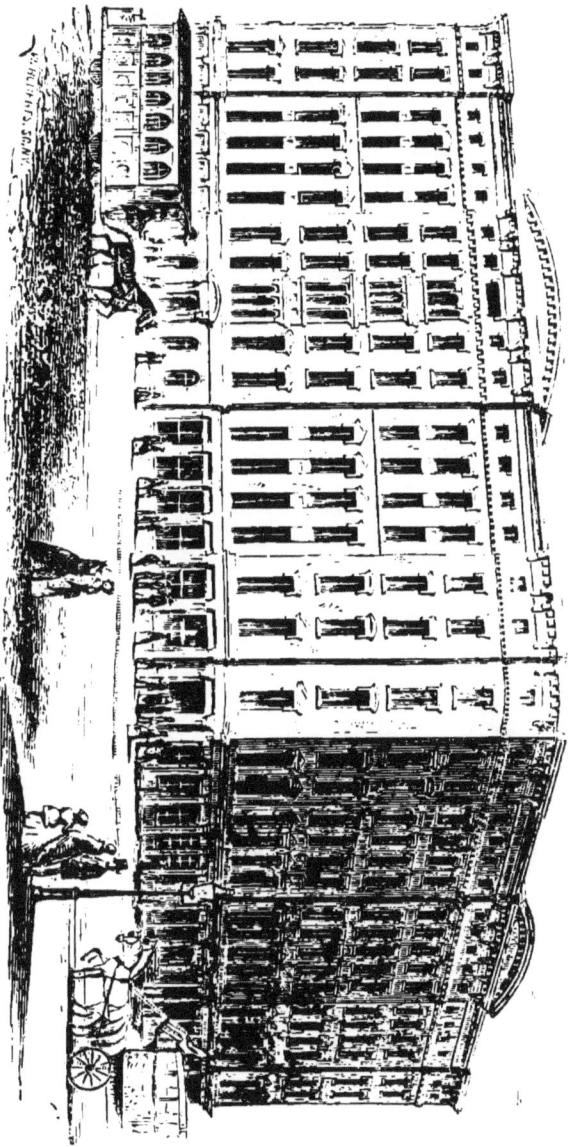

TONTINE HOUSE 1st at Wall Street, New York

quarters of an acre of ground, stands the Bible House. It is the property of the American Bible Society, and cost, in building about $300,000.

The society was organized in 1816, and the receipts for the first year were $37,779 35 ; and 6.410 Bibles were issued. During the past year, $677.851 36 were received, and 1,530,563 Bibles and Testaments distributed.

The work of distribution never ceases. In the cellars and garrets of the poor, in our great cities, in the distant and solitary cabins of the new Territories, in the mining regions, glittering with gold and reeking with wickedness, on the frontiers, where savages have slaughtered the helpless settlers, in the lonesome military posts of the far North west, among the rich and the poor in every part of the land, among emigrants, upon the ship and the dock, the good work goes bravely forward.

Hundreds of thousands of poverty-stricken families and individuals, to-day, but for the direct efforts of the society, would not possess a Bible or Testament, and not one of hundreds of thousands more has been refused because of inability to purchase the precious treasure.

Bibles, or portions of the Bible, have been published in twenty-six different languages or dialects. Editions of the holy book are sent to Europe, Asia and Africa ; neither have the Choctaw, Ojibwa, Cherokee, Mohawk, and other North American Indians been forgotten.

In the building of the Bible House, the annexed societies have their offices : The Protestant Episcopal Society, for the Promotion of Evangelical Knowledge ; the American Board of Commissioners for Foreign Missions ; the American Home Missionary Society ; the New York Colonization Society ; Society for the Amelioration of the Condition of the Jews ; the House of Refuge ; Children's Aid Society and Home of the Friendless.

In the same building, on the Third avenue side, is the Young Men's Christian Association, where devotional services are held on Wednesday and Saturday evenings. Strangers are cordially invited to attend.

At the corner of Eleventh street and Second avenue stands

the New York Historical Society, estaolished upwards of fifty years. It is built of yellow sandstone, and is considered fireproof. No strangers are permitted to enter, unless provided with tickets of admission, procurable from one of the members. The society boasts of a library of about 20,000 volumes ; a picture gallery, and a splendid collection of Nineveh marbles and Egyptian antiquities.

The Free Academy, at the corner of Lexington avenue and Twenty-third street, is under the control of the Board of Education. It was established in 1848, in pursuance of an act passed in 1847, for the purpose of providing higher education to those pupils of the common schools who wish to avail themselves of the privilege. Though under the control of the Board of Education, an Executive Committee is appointed by that body, and are responsible for its proper care and management. As its name indicates, it is a free institution, and the expenses for instruction, books, stationery, &c., are paid from the State appropriation.

The full course of study embraces a period of five years ; at the end of that time, the Board of Education is authorized, by law, to confer degrees on those scholars who have passed the proper examination.

It is arranged for the accommodation of a hundred pupils, who, when they graduate, can become what is termed Resident Graduates, and continue their course of studies. The cost of the building, including ground-rent, was nearly one hundred and fifty thousand dollars.

The National Academy of Design occupies the whole of a lot, situated at the north-west corner of Fourth avenue and Twenty-third street, eighty feet wide on the street, and ninety-eight feet nine inches long on the avenue. It is three stories high, besides the cellar. The lower story contains the Janitor's apartments, the floor of which is raised one step above the sidewalk occupying the whole end on Twenty-third street, and the rooms of the School of Design, the floor of which is four feet lower than that of the Janitor's rooms ; thus giving a ceiling sixteen feet high, and which occupy three-fourths of the whole basement story. The accommodations for the school are ample. It occupies three studios, or alcoves, on Fourth avenue, lighted by large windows, and a hall for casts and models, the whole covering a space of forty-seven by sixty-eight feet. The Life-School occupies a hall, in the north side of the building twenty-seven by fifty-four feet, and partially lighted from a court-yard. *The entrance to all the rooms on this story is by a door in the southern end of the Fourth avenue side.

The principal story is reached by a double flight of steps, on the Twenty-third street end, and is entered by a large doorway, from which a hall, eighteen feet wide, runs nearly the whole length of the building. The whole Fourth avenue side is occupied by a suite of four rooms ; the most southerly is the Reception room, twenty-two by twenty-six feet ; the next two, each the same size as the reception room, are for the Library. The most northerly is the Council Room, which is twenty-two by forty five feet. To the west of the Central Hall are ladies' and gentlemen's dressing-rooms, and a Lecture room, which is immediately above, and the same size as the Life School room, in the story below.

On the upper story are the Exhibition Galleries. In the centre is a hall thirty-four by forty feet, divided by a double arcade, supported on columns of polished marble. In this hall are hung the works of Art belonging to the National Academy. Around this are the Galleries, all opening out of it ; one thirty by seventy-six feet ; one twenty-two by forty-six; one twenty by forty ; one twenty by thirty—all lighted by sky-lights ; also a gallery for Sculpture, twenty-one feet square, lighted both from the roof and the side.

Visitors to the Galleries enter at the main entrance, in the first story. On the left of a person so entering, is the ticket office ; on the right, the umbrella depository. Passing through the vestibule, the visitor enters the Great Hall ; in front are *the stairs leading up to the Galleries above ; four steps. the whole width of the hall, lead to a platform, where he gives up his ticket and purchases his catalogue ; from this a double flight leads to another platform, from which a single flight reaches the level of the Gallery floor.

These stairs, together with all the doors, door and window
trimmings, mantels, &c., are of oak and walnut combined,
oiled and polished. The halls and vestibules are floored with
mosaic.

On the exterior, the walls of the basement story are of West-
chester County gray marble, with bands of North River gray-
wacke. The walls of the first story are of white marble, with
similar bands ; and of the third story of white and gray marble,
in small oblong blocks, forming a pattern of chequer work.
The building is surmounted by a rich arcade cornice of white
marble.

The School of Design, in the basement, is lighted by wide
double windows, with segmental arches, each pair of arches supported in the middle on a clustered column, with a rich carved
capital and base, and resting on each side on a carved corbel.
All the other windows in the building have pointed arches, and
those of the first story have their archivolts decorated by
voussoirs of alternately white and gray marble. There are
no windows in the upper story upon the street, but circular
openings for ventilation, filled with elaborate plate tracery.
The principal entrance is very nigh. A broad archivolt, en-
riched with sculpture and varied by voussoirs, alternately white
and gray, springs from columns, two on each side, of red Ver-
mont marble, with white marble capitals and bases. The
double flight of steps leading to this door, is an important
feature of the building, being entirely of marble, hav ng under
the platform, a triple arcade, inclosing a drinking fountain, and
being richly decorated with sculpture.

The style of architecture is revived Gothic, now the domi-
nant style in England, and combines those features of the
different schools of architecture of the middle ages.

Taken altogether, it is a quaint and elegant structure, and
was erected at the cost of about $150,000. P. B. Wright, Esq.
was the architect. The annual exhibitions of the Academy
take place during the months of April, May, June and July, to
which the public are admitted on payment of a small admission
fee. In these exhibitions living artists are only represented,
and no pictures are allowed to be shown that have previously
been exhibited in New York.

During the months of November and December, annually, the Artists' Fund Society is held here, when another exhibition of pictures takes place. The proceeds are devoted to the relief of sick and indigent artists.

On Thirtieth street, between Fourth and Madison avenues, stands The House of Industry and Home for the Friendless. Its object is the protection of deserted children, and adult persons who need relief; it is an excellent society, and in one year relieved and found places for over 600 persons. In its interest is published a paper called *The Advocate and Guardian*, issued semi-monthly, which has a circulation of 15,000 copies.

Some few years ago the attention of Dr. J. D. Russ was called to the helpless and sightless condition of a number of children who were occupants of the City Alms-House. Pained at the sight, he benevolently determined to do something for their relief, and to that end took seven children from the Alms-House, and instructed them, gratuitously, for nearly two years, when he obtained from the Legislature the passage of an act for their support.

In this laudable undertaking he was nobly and ably supported by a well known member of the Society of Friends, Samuel Wood; also by Dr. Samuel Akerly, well known for his well directed energy in behalf of the Deaf and Dumb Asylum.

Finally, The Institution for the Blind, on Ninth avenue, between Thirty-third and Thirty-fourth streets, was erected. It occupies thirty-two lots of ground which were presented by James Boorman, Esq.

It is one of the most interesting institutions in the city to visit, which can be done every day, except Sundays, between the hours of 1 and 6 P.M. The pupils are taught to read, and are instructed in several useful branches of trade.

From the Blind Asylum to that of the Deaf and Dumb is a natural transition. It is one of the best conducted and best endowed charitable institutions in New York, and is situated at Fanwood, Washington Heights, near One Hundred and Fiftieth street. Two to three hundred pupils are constantly being instructed therein in reading, writing and the ordinary rudiments of an English education. Besides this, they are taught

useful and various branches of industry. Dr. Pease is the effi-
cient Superintendent ; visitors are admitted from half-past 1
to 4 p. m., every day.

Among the many admirable institutions that New York can
boast, none has done more good, or been productive of more
beneficial results than the Magdalen Female Asylum, located
west of the Harlem Railroad, between Eigh.ty-eighth and
Eighty-ninth streets. As its name denotes, it is intended for
the reformation and restoration to society of those poor unfortunate females who have erred from the paths of virtue. It is
well sustained, and by its exertions many have been restored
to the means of gaining an honest livelihood.

At Bloomingdale, near Eightieth street, is The New York
Orphan Asylum. From the grounds of which institution a
beautiful view can be obtained of the Hudson and East Rivers,
the Palisades and surrounding scenery. It received its first
charter in 1807, and the present building, 160 feet long by 60
feet wide, was erected in 1840. About 200 orphans are regularly provided for in this Asylum.

There is also another Orphan Asylum, on One Hundred and
Seventeenth street, between Fourth and Fifth avenues. It
was founded by two charitable personages whose name it bears,
viz: The Leake and Watts Orphan Asylum. The grounds com-
prise about twenty-six acres, and are laid out with much taste.

Besides the Hospitals, already mentioned, thére are the
Jew's Hospital, located at 158 West Twenty-eighth street ; St.
Luke's Hospital, corner of Fifth avenue and Fiftieth street,
under the auspices of the Episcopal churches of New York ;
and the Children's Hospital and Nursery on Fifty-first street,
near Lexington avenue.

The University Medical School is on Fourteenth street, between Irving Place and Third avenue, to which is attached a
most valuable and extensive museum.

At the corner of Twenty-third street and Fourth avenue is
The College of Physicians and Surgeons, founded in 1807. In
it are an anatomical museum, and a small but valuable medical
library of nearly 1600 volumes. These can be visited by
making application to the janitor.

No. 90 East Thirteenth street is the building known as The New York Medical College, to which is attached the College of Pharmacy, both of which are devoted to the instruction of medical students.

The New York Medical Institute is at No. 8 Union Square, and is devoted almost exclusively to the science of electricity. As a remedial agent, electricity has been little known, but since the establishment of this institute it has been found that its vitalizing effects are wonderful, and that in all pulmonary and renal complaints it is invaluable.

As well as all these hospitals are The New York Dispensaries, established for giving medical advice and medicine to that class of poor who are not sick enough, or, who do not wish to obtain admittance into a hospital. The oldest one was established in 1795, and is on the corner of White and Centre streets; the Northern Dispensary, on the corner of Christopher and Sixth streets, was instituted in 1829, and the Eastern Dispensary, on the corner of Ludlow street and Essex Market Place, was founded in 1834. It is estimated that between five and six thousand persons are annually benefitted at these dispensaries.

In the building, at the corner of Second avenue and Twenty-third street, is The Demilt Dispensary, which, with the gound, was donated by the late Miss Demilt, at the cost of $80,000.

Bellevue Hospital, occupying the entire block on First avenue, between Twenty-sixth and Twenty-seventh streets, is under the control of the Commissioners of Charities and Corrections, and is of inestimable benefit to the poor of New York. It is capable of holding one thousand beds.

Under the direct daily superintendence of the most distinguished surgeons and physicians of the city, supplied with every remedy for disease, and every comfort, the poor and friendless have all the advantages in the treatment of disease that the most affluent can command.

Whether tested by the number of patients, by the variety of the forms of disease, or the percentage of successful operations and cures, there is no institution in Europe or in this country that excels Bellevue Hospital in public usefulness.

Nor do its benefits end here; as a school of instruction to

the students of the several medical colleges, it is of great and
permanent value, for here can be learned, under the tuition of
the most skillful physicians and surgeons, the proper treatment
of disease in all its forms, and the best modes of performing
operations.

On the 1st of April last, a medical department for the treatment of the Out-Door Sick Poor was established, and provision
made for the treatment of cases of general medicine and
general surgery, and in the specialties of diseases of the eye
and ear, of the skin, of the nervous system, and diseases of the
chest.

This was done, as it was found that a large class of patients
who sought admission to the hospital might be as advanta-
geously treated as out-door patients, and the hospital thus be
relieved from the burthen of their maintenance, and that many
suffering from maladies which did not incapacitate them from
pursuing their usual vocations, but who are unable to pay for
the services of skillful physicians, or for expensive medicines,
would avail themselves of this mode of relief.

Annexed is a table showing the number of persons admitted
in the hospital during the year 1865 :

Number of patients admitted................7,073
Of which died........................... 658
Discharged cured...... 5,801
Remaining................... 614
                                        ———
                                        7,073

The daily cost of treating each in-door patient is a trifle over
thirty-nine cents per day.

Our next visit is to Blackwell's Island, on which are a Hospital, a Penitentiary, Alms-Houses, Work-House, and a Lunatic
Asylum

The Hospital is situated on the southerly end of Blackwell's
Island, and holds 1,200 beds. It embraces all the improve-
ments in heating and ventilation, and its general internal
arrangements are unsurpassed by any hospital in the United
States. During the past year radical changes have been made
in the organization of the employees.

Previous to the 16th of May, 1865, it was in charge of the warden of the Penitentiary, and the nurses and orderlies were Work-House prisoners. The wards were filthy, and drunkenness and riot were of frequent occurrence. On the 16th of May, a resident warden was appointed, who returned to the work-house the prisoners acting as orderlies and nurses, and appointed, at moderate wages, respectable and competent persons in their stead.

An instant improvement was observable, the wards were cleaned, turbulence and drunkenness disappeared, economy and individual responsibility were introduced, and now the hospital will compare favorably with any other institution in the world in cleanliness, order, and the attention and devotion of its employees.

The greater portion of the patients are afflicted with a loathsome disease, and it is apprehended that with the increase of the population of the city, this class of patients will increase, and that it will be necessary either to assign this hospital, or to build one for their exclusive treatment.

Subjoined is a statement of the number of patients treated during the past year.

Number of patients..................... 9,877
Died..................... 744
Cured.... 8,157
Remaining....................... 976

_____

9,877

The average daily cost of patients received in this hospital, is about twenty-nine cents.

Since the close of the war, the number of prisoners confined in the Penitentiary have greatly increased. In 1864, only 921 were confined, while in 1865, the number swelled to 1,670. It is believed there will be a large increase this year.

The system of prison discipline is defective. Instead of reforming persons convicted of crime, it is admitted, that the present discipline, by its harsh and undiscriminating character, confirms the prisoner in his criminal pursuits, and, on his discharge from prison. he is prepared for the commission of graver crimes than when he entered.

At several of the European prisons there has been a radical change in the system of prison discipline, and the change seems to have been followed by the hap, iest results. A large portion of the convicts, under the influence of the new system of discrimination, have, it is alleged, been entirely reformed, and have become orderly citizens.

The experiment of the new system, however, has been too recent to warrant its general introduction into the prisons of the State ; yet, the evidences of improvement are sufficiently authentic to justify the trial to a limited extent.

In the Alms Houses, on Blackwell's Island, on the 1st of January, 1865, were 1,497 persons, and there were received during the year, 3,590 more persons, making a total of 5,087 persons. Of these, 2,682 were discharged, 823 died, and 1,582 remain.

Among the most difficult problems of social science, is the proper mode and measure of relief for the poor and friendless. The indiscriminate aid through public officers, to all persons in want, is sure to encourage idleness and beggary, while the total withdrawal of support would increase the mass of wretchedness and crime. There can be no doubt, if the remedy were adequate, the poor would be more judiciously assisted by private charity than through the means of public relief.

The examination into the circumstances of each individual case is more thorough ; the opportunities for fraud are lessened ; the measure of relief more readily and accurately ascertained ; nor is the recipient degraded in his own esteem, by receiving aid from private sources. The inmate of an alms house loses all self-reliance, if not self-respect, when the doors close upon him.

Hence private hospitals, asylums, retreats for the old and infirm should be encouraged, as being not only the most effective and economical modes of relief, but, above all, because they strengthen the bonds of sympathy between the rich and the poor, between the donor and recipient.

But, unhappily, the charity of the rich is not commensurate with the wants of the poor, and the deficiency must be supplemented by contributions from the public funds. The regulations established before persons can be admitted into the Alms House, or obtain out-door relief, are as stringent as is compatible with the ends for which this Commission was created ; yet many obtain aid who have either means of their own, or who have relatives abundantly able to support them. It requires constant vigilance, by the officers employed, to detect and punish these frauds.

The Workhouse is used as a reformatory for vagrants and drunkards, with the rigorous discipline of the penitentiary, without its degrading associations, and has fulfilled, under the able administration of Mr. Fitch, the purposes for which it was intended. During the past year, 12,346 persons were committed to his care.

The next, and last building to visit on Blackwell's Island, is the Lunatic Asylum. It is probable that no similar institution in the country is as much visited as this ; and everything is being done, through motives of humanity, interest and pride, to make it the model asylum of its kind in the world.

In 1865, there were 1,284 lunatics treated at the Asylum ; of these, 421 were discharged, 127 died, and 736 are remaining.

Here, on Randall's Island, are the nurseries for the reception of vagrant and helpless children. They are objects of increasing interest and usefulness, and are the homes of abandoned children, or of children whose parents are unable to support them, or of widows living at service, who can make little or no provision for their care, though, so far as their ability will permit, the parents or relatives are required to pay for their support.

Aside from the dictates of humanity, requiring that provision should be made for abandoned and foundling children, the public interests are deeply involved ; for, it is ascertained, that of the convicts of the State, 32 per cent. were, in childhood, either orphans or half-orphans.

Under the supervision of the Wardens, and of intelligent and kind matrons, the children are clothed and fed, and educated, and thus rescued from the contamination of evil associations in the streets of a great city.

When they arrive at a proper age, they are apprenticed to

some industrial pursuit, and become useful citizens. It is difficult to over-estimate the positive good derived from these public nurseries.

Every day affords evidence of their supreme importance, as
a refuge for children without the moral restraint of parental
care. Here, distributed according to their ages, in small families, they are tenderly watched by the matrons, and are subject
to all the kindly influences of well-regulated homes.

There are sixty idiot children on Randall's Island, and a
separate building is assigned to them, but no attempts have
hitherto been made to develop their latent reason. Application has been made to Doctor Wilbur, the principal of the
State Asylum for Idiots, for a competent teacher, and it is
hoped that, by the employment of the same means, the same
gratifying results may be obtained as have distinguished Dr.
Wilbur's efforts in behalf of this unfortunate class.

Permits for visiting Blackwell's or Randall's Island can be
obtained of Mr. George Kellock, Superintendent of Out-door
Poor, No. 1 Bond street.

WALK THE FOURTH.

NEWSPAPER OFFICES.

Jonathan was ahead of me this morning.

When I descended to the breakfast-room, I found him already there, waiting for me. Apparently he was pleased as a child with a new toy, and on my entering the room, he looked slyly at his watch, and asked me if I was tired.

" Tired ! not a bit. Why do you ask ? ''

"Oh, nothing !'' and he again, with a facetious twinkle in his eye, consulted his watch.

"Come, out with it,'' said I laughing ; "I see you have something to say, so out with it.''

" I. was thinking, John, that if you felt tired to-day we would not go out. It is true my stay in the city is not long, but I would rather miss seeing some of the sights than distress an old friend.''

The serious-comic manner with which he said this was inimitable.

" Why, you old humbug,'' I replied, " because you are a few minutes ahead of me this morning, you try to make it appear I am worn out with our travels.''

" No, no ! not at all ; it is simply my extreme solicitude for your health.''

" Now I see through it,'' I exclaimed. " You are worn out yourself, and don't feel like walking, and want to throw the blame of an excuse upon me.'' •

" No, really I do not,'' replied Jonathan earnestly ; " I like walking, it does me good,'' here he inflated his chest ; " but you have chided me every morning for keeping you waiting, so I thought I would have a little joke about my being first. And you know I must have my joke.''

If Jonathan had said he must have his little choke he would have been nearer correct, for chuckling over his own facetiousness a piece of breakfast biscuit went the wrong way, and he coughed and spluttered in a manner painful to behold. I went to his assistance and restored him to his normal condition by administering a few severe thumps upon his back.

"Where are you thinking of taking me to this day?" queried Jonathan.

"To-day we will devote our attention to newspaper offices and as soon as you have stowed away sufficient cargo we wil start."

This was my jocose way of saying "when you have finishec breakfast."

"I am ready," said Jonathan, rising and brushing the crumbs from his lap with a napkin.

"Then off we go," and in a few minutes we started.

Getting into a stage to ride down town we obtained seats near the further end. I had the twenty cents ready, and before Jonathan noticed it had handed them to the driver.

Soon another passenger got in, and seated himself near the door, who handed ten cents to Jonathan for him to give to the driver.

I observed that Jonathan gazed with a surprised and bewildered look at the stamp, and heard him mumble something to himself, but beyond that I took no further notice.

Presently the driver began thumping most vigorously on the top of the stage, much to Jonathan's annoyance, who told me that he thought it disgraceful for the man to make so much noise. Finally the driver, when he found his stock of thumps exhausted, shouted through the hole, "that some man in there had not paid his fare."

No one took the slightest notice.

"Are you going to pay me that fare?" asked Jehu.

"Go on driver," shouted a passenger, "everybody's paid."

"No they haven't. That gentleman who last got in, and who is sitting near the door, hasn't paid."

All eyes were turned toward the gentleman indicated.

"Yes I have," said that individual, and frowning to Jonathan he continued: "You remember, sir, I handed you my fare to pass up, on entering the stage."

Jonathan turned all manner of colors, muttered something perfectly unintelligible, drew a ten cent stamp from his waistcoat pocket and handed it to the driver.

"A queer old chap that," said the gentleman, as he alighted from the stage, alluding to Jonathan.

By this time we had reached the City Hall Park, so we, also got out. When we had done so, I said to Griggs, "Why did you pay that fellow's fare?"

"To tell you the truth, John, I never was so mortified in all my life. I will explain to you why. When that man handed me the ten cents—"

"Oh! then, he did give you the money?"

"Yes, of course. And when he did so, I thought he intended to insult me, by offering me money; but why he should do so, I could not define, so, determining to punish him for his insolence, I took the money and put it in my pocket."

I laughed heartily at Jonathan's mode of resenting an insult.

"Did you not know that it was a common occurrence for people sitting near the door of a stage, to hand their fare to the person nearest the driver, for them to hand it to him?"

"How should I? When I left the city, New York was not the New York it is to-day, and stages were not. But I assure you, I never felt so ashamed in all my life. When that man said he had given me the money to pay his fare, I wished myself anywhere but in that stage."

Seeing that Jonathan's feelings really were hurt, I changed the conversation.

"There are," I said, "published daily, in New York, about fifteen papers, with an aggregate circulation of about 300,000 copies."

"My gracious! as many as that?"

"It is impossible to get at a correct estimate, but I presume it amounts to that. Publishers, as a rule, are so jealous of their circulation, that they tell none of its secrets, and guard it with as much care as a husband would his wife, or a lover his sweetheart."

"This number, I presume, includes both English and foreign?"

" Yes ; English, French, and German. The principal English papers are the *Herald*, *Times*, *Tribune*, *World*, *Post*, and
Express ; the two last being evening papers."

By this time we had crossed the Park, and now stood in
Printing House Square.

" Is that *The Tribune ?"* asked Jonathan. " Horace Greeley's
paper ?"

" Yes; that is the celebrated Horace Greeley's paper, and
stands, as you see, at the corner of Spruce and Nassau streeets.
This fine, handsome building, facing Chatham street, is the
Times office. It is the finest newspaper building in the city, indeed, I might say, in the whole United States."

" It is a magnificent edifice, certainly."

" The *Herald*, which now stands on the corner of Fulton and
Nassau streets, is shortly to be removed to the corner of Ann
and Broadway. The building is not yet completed, but rumor
says it is going to be a model edifice of its kind."

"I presume Bennett will endeavor to beat the *Times* in the
elegance of his building. Competition is a great thing."

" I should not be at all surprised. But let us, as the French
say, return to our muttons. The *Times* building was erected in
1857, a year memorable in the commercial history of this city,
as the panic year. The site was formerly occupied by the old
Brick Church, erected when this portion of the city was considered out of town. When the church and ground were sold,
Government talked of buying it, and building a post office
thereon."

" It appears to me, that no better location could have been
selected."

" It would have answered the purpose admirably. But the
proprietors of the *Times* wanting it for their own use, bought it
over the heads of the Government officials."

" It must have cost a good round sum ?"

" About $300,000, I believe ; a much less sum than it could
be purchased for now."

"Can we examine the building ?"

"Oh, yes. When we have gone through the *Times* building
it will answer for the whole, as the prominent features in all
large newspaper offices are the same."

Entering the building, we made known our wishes, and was immediately placed in the hands of a guide, who, at once, began to show and explain to us objects of interest.

On the ground floor is the counting-room, where advertisements are received. On the right of the counting-room, as you enter from Printing House Square, is the cashier's office ; through that little window in the glass case that contains the cashier, the hearts of the editorial and reportorial *attachés* are gladdened every Friday afternoon.

On the left is the mail clerk, who is also engaged inclosed in a glass case. From appearances, the proprietors of the *Times* think a good deal of their clerks, they take so much care of them ; or, else they adopt the forcing system, and keep them under glass, to more fully develop them.

The duties of this clerk are, to receive all letters that are received at the *Times* office. A boy fetches them from the Post Office, but as the majority of them contain money, they are put into a tin box, which is securely locked, a key for that purpose being kept at the post office, and a duplicate one by the mail-clerk.

"These," said our guide, pointing to a heap of letters that were being rapidly opened by the mail-clerk, "are letters containing subscriptions for our weekly, semi-weekly, or daily. It is the business of this gentleman to see they are properly entered into the subscription books, and that when the term of subscription expires, to see that the paper is no longer sent unless re-subscribed for "

" Quite a task for one man," said Jonathan.

" Yes ; but, then, the business is so well organized, that seldom or never does a mistake occur. In this room are the wrapper-writers, whose only occupation, during the entire day, is to write the addresses of subscribers."

" A somewhat monotonous job."

" Not more so than copying, generally. Now, before visiting the press-room, we will ascend to the third story, and examine the editorial rooms."

" Will Mr. Raymond be there?" inquired Jonathan. " I should like to see him."

" He is at present in Washington ; his duties, as a Member of Congress, calling h'm there."

" A Member of Congress ! and still edits this paper ?" ejaculated Jonathan, surprised.

" Oh, yes. In Mr. Raymond's absence, the paper is under the control of the managing editor, who is thoroughly instructed in the line of conduct the paper should pursue ; so there is little danger of his going wrong."

After being shown the editorial rooms, Mr. Raymond's private room, and the library, which is well stored with books of reference, we were taken to the reporters' room, on the same floor. By the reporters the city news is obtained.

Jonathan was under the impression, that reporters procured news by walking about the streets, and that whenever they saw an incident or a murder, they rushed forward, got all the particulars, and published them.

But when told that each reporter had his especial duty to attend to, and that his business for the day was arranged for him by a gentleman, called the City Editor, he was much astonished.

" On the fourth story is the composing room—the best appointed, the best lighted, and most commodious one in the city. Compositors are constantly employed, day and night ; they are ever busy, no idleness being permitted for a moment." Thus spoke our guide.

Jonathan murmured something about the busy bee.

" If, as frequently happens, there is no copy for the men to go on with, they are made to work on setting up ' dead ' matter. That is, composition never intended to be printed."

" But why is that done ?"

" For this reason : if there was no work for the men, they would not stay in the office. In a daily newspaper office important telegraphic news may be received at any moment, that would necessitate the publishing of an extra edition ; so it is absolutely necessary to find the men employment."

On the left of the composing room, is the stereotyping department. Here, when the paper is all set up, two stereotypes are taken of each form—occupying rather less than twenty minutes of time—thus enabling two presses to throw off copies of the same form at once."

"That must be a great advantage."

"It is ; for it allows us to go to press at a much later hour, which was an invaluable boon during the war, and even now has great advantages upon the late arrival of European news."

"Just so."

"Besides this, something had to be done to enable us to print a sufficient number to meet the demands of our increasing circulation."

We next descended to the vaults ; they are the finest and most commodious ever constructed in New York, and extend on Spruce street, one hundred by twenty-six feet ; on Park Row one hundred by twenty feet ; on Nassau street ninety-five by fifteen feet, and are twenty-four feet deep. On the Park Row side is the store-room for paper ; on the Nassau street side are two immense boilers—large enough for an ocean steamer— used for running the presses, of which there are two.

One is a ten cylinder, the other a six cylinder press ; they are known as Hoe's lightning presses, and at each turn of the cylinder the former prints ten papers, the latter six.

"John," said Jonathan, "I have arrived at the conclusion, there is a vast deal of difference between running a paper in this city and out in the town I come from."

I was also of opinion there was some difference.

"There," he continued, "the editor among other odd jobs helps to set type and collect advertisements, and who, with the assistance of a boy, prints the whole edition upon a hand press, and delivers it to the subscribers."

' "Now we will pay a visit to Torrey Brothers' establishment, No. 13 Spruce street."

"What are they ?"

"I am astonished. Do neither circuses nor shows ever visit your benighted town ?"

"Of course they do. But what has that to do with my question ?"

"A great deal. Have you not noticed before the arrival of

a show that your town was gaily decorated with many colored wood cuts and posters?''

"I have, and often examined them with a good deal of curiosity."

"Then did you never notice the imprint of Torrey Brothers upon them?''

"Let me consider. Why, yes, of course I have."

"I thought so, for that firm are printers of the majority of such show bills and posters. However, it is not the printing office I wish you to examine, but the subterranean establishment of Messrs. Torrey & Green."

"The subterranean establishment!" exclaimed Jonathan, doubting if he had heard correctly.

"Yes. Do you see those buildings on either side of the street?''

"If it is not an optical delusion, I do."

"In each of those buildings machinery of some kind is used; also in the corresponding block of Beekman street, which is below, and the corresponding block of Frankfort street, which is above. For all this machinery the running power is obtained from the engines of Messrs. Torrey & Green, who were the originators of the plan for supplying motive power to machinery from engines situated a block off."

"You don't tell me."

Descending into the engine-room, Jonathan expressed his admiration of the engines, of which there are two, and was lost in wonderment at the fly wheel, which is 48 feet in circumference.

At this juncture we heard the shrill shriek of the steam whistle; in an instant the engine-room was deserted, save by one man, and there was a patter and clatter of many feet above.

"What, what's the matter; is it fire?''

The man to whom this question was addressed, laughed.

"No; it is half-past 12, dinner hour; and the boys belonging to the various offices are anxious to get out into the street to play."

"Dinner hour!" said Jonathan. "I am hungry; let us go and have some lunch."

So we went to Crook, Fox & Nash's restaurant, Nos. 40 and 41 Park Row, and satisfied the cravings of our appetites.

"Here," said I to Jonathan, "may be seen a sight that cannot be witnessed in any other than a Republican country."

"How so?"

"You see the throng that is now collected here, doing as we have just now done. Well, it is composed of editors, literary men, artists, politicians, merchants, their clerks, the millionare and the man who has hardly a penny to bless himself with. The poor man is jostling the rich man, and Republican and Democrat are quietly sitting side by side, as though there was no such thing as politics, and parties were unknown. Talk of the lion and the lamb lying down together, why, it's nothing to it."

"Ah! it's a great country," was all that Jonathan said.

WALK THE FIFTH.

PUBLIC AMUSEMENTS.

I have no doubt that my readers will now accuse me of a Hibernianism, for this chapter is called a walk, and there is no more pedestrianism in it than there is grass on Broadway.

However, there is one consolation, it is not my fault. If any blame is attached to anybody it is solely to Jonathan. So you will please pour out your vials of wrath upon his head, and not mine.

I will endeavor to explain how it is his fault.

It was my intention to visit a theatre every evening of Jonathan's stay with me, but he had the happy faculty of getting so completely tired out during the day, that he was fit for nothing in the evening, but bed.

Now, be it known, I take a great interest in dramatic entertainments of all kinds, and felt sorry that Jonathan would have to leave the city without visiting one of our leading theatres.

I thought of the chagrin he would experience, upon his return home, when asked about any place of public amusement, at not being able to answer it. This state of deplorable ignorance would recoil upon me. He would be asked who was his friend, counsellor and guide in New York, and he would have to answer John Wetherby.

This would never do, so I made out a list of the various theatres with a brief account of the style of entertainment to be found at each. Here they are.

ACADEMY OF MUSIC.—This splendid theatre, the largest in New York, is situated at the corner of Irving Place and Fourteenth street. It is devoted almost exclusively to music— during the season operas being given three or four times a week. Opera is one of the fashionable amusements of New

York, consequently the building is generally well filled with what is called the *elite* of society. Whether this is brought about by the deep love our citizens have for music, or a strong yearning to exhibit their good clothes—for, be it known, you are nothing unless full dressed—I will not determine. Certain it is, the fact is as I have stated. It is capable of accommodating about four thousand persons.

IRVING HALL.—Exactly opposite the Academy of Music, on Irving Place, is the most fashionable music hall in the city. Mr. Lafayette Harrison is the proprietor and manager, and has well earned the deserved title of being the best caterer for the amusement of the public in the city. During the winter months, when balls are all the rage, many of the best are given here. No matter what the style of entertainment, whether a concert, ball, or lecture, it is safe to depend upon a pleasant evening's amusement.

WALLACK'S THEATRE.—Now under the management of Mr. Lester Wallack, the best light comedian in the country, is located at the corner of Thirteenth street and Broadway. Its style of entertainment is varied, consisting of comedy, melodrama and farce. No matter what the play, it is sure to be better put upon the stage, and acted with more artistic finish than at any other house in town. It is celebrated for the reproduction of old comedies—plays that our fathers, and their father's fathers laughed over. For a quiet, pleasant evening's amusement, no place is more likely to afford it than this.

WINTER GARDEN—Under the La Farge House, and opposite Bond street, on Broadway, it is one of the most conveniently situated theatres for pleasure-seekers. The class of entertainment offered at this house ranges "from grave to gay, from lively to severe." Shakespeare's tragedy of *Hamlet*, in which Mr. Edwin Booth appeared, was so beautifully acted by that gentleman, and so charmingly placed upon the stage, that it ran for a hundred consecutive nights—a triumph unknown in the annals of the drama. Bulwer's play of *Richelieu*, in which the

same actor represented the Cardinal Duke, was also mounted
so superbly, that both the press and public went almost crazy
with delight.   It was an epoch in dramatic history, and reflects
great credit on the enterprise and liberality of the management.

OLYMPIC THEATRE.—This charming theatre is under the management of Mrs. John Wood, the most pleasing, vivacious and
jolly actress on the stage.   Vaudevilles, farces and burlesques
are usually the attractions at this house, which are always
placed upon the stage with due attention to scenic surroundings.   For a man afflicted with the blues, there is no place better adapted to dispel them than here.   All are sure of a hearty
laugh, for Mrs. John Wood's comic powers are irresistible.   She
well deserves the enviable title of Queen of Comedy.   It is
situated at 622 Broadway.

BARNUM'S MUSEUM.—Among the many places of amusement
in New York, none are so popular with country people as Barnum's Museum.   When the old building, at the corner of Ann
street and Broadway, was burned down, Mr. Barnum, in an incredible short space of time, fitted up the old Chinese Assembly
Rooms, located on Broadway, between Spring and Prince streets,
as a museum.   The admission is only thirty cents ; and a more
diversified entertainment cannot be procured anywhere.   Here
may be seen giants, dwarfs, serpents, monkeys, three-horned
bulls, and almost every description of curiosity the mind of
man can imagine.   Besides all this, there are dramatic entertainments in the lecture-room, every afternoon and evening.

WOOD'S THEATRE is exactly opposite the St. Nicholas Hotel,
and is well patronized by pleasure-seekers.   It was formerly a
Negro Minstrel Hall, and has only lately been converted into a
theatre.

BROADWAY THEATRE.—This theatre, one door from Broome
street, on the west side of Broadway, is well worthy a visit, as
a pleasing evening's entertainment is sure to be obtained here.
It has been the scene of many histrionic triumphs, the latest of

which is Mr. John Owens', who played the character of *Solon Shingle*, in "The People's Lawyer," for nearly four hundred nights.

BOWERY THEATRE—As its name indicates, stands on the Bowery, near Canal street, and is celebrated for its spectacle pieces and pantomimes. Mr. G. L. Fox, the manager, is one of the best dumb clowns on the stage. The manner in which he expresses the various emotions of love, hope, fear, cunning, ambition and revenge, simply by contortions of the face and body, is unapproachable, and must be seen to be appreciated.

NEW BOWERY THEATRE.—This popular place of amusement is also on the Bowery, near Hester street. The blue and red fire school of melo-drama holds almost undisputed sway here, as that class of entertainment best pleases its patrons.

NEW YORK STADT THEATRE—Is nearly opposite the Bowery Theatre. The plays are in German, and are well supported by the German population.

NEGRO MINSTRELSY.—The principal and best halls for Ethiopean Minstrelsy, are the Bryant's 472 Broadway ; San Francisco, opposite the Metropolitan Hotel, and George Christy's, on Twenty-fourth street, under the Fifth avenue Hotel.

WALK THE SIXTH.

WHARVES AND SHIPPING.

"To-day," said I to Jonathan, when we had finished our matutinal repast, " I intend giving you some idea of the vast commercial importance of the city of New York."

" Nothing I should like better," replied Griggs, rubbing his hands, " how do you intend doing it, for my ideas are pretty thoroughly fixed upon that point already."

"I have no doubt of it, but they will be more strongly planted when you have seen the ceaseless activity along the wharves, and examined the shipping and ship yards."

"That may be John, but I am somewhat dubious ; for my opinion at present is, there is no city like this in the world. I may be right, or I may be wrong, but that is my opinion."

" We will see."

So we set out upon our pilgrimage. Riding down town I conducted Jonathan to the foot of the North River, and commenced my harrangue as follows :

"Here, at Pier No. 1, is the landing place of the boats belonging to the Camden and Amboy Railroad, the first line built running South from New York. When the road was first built it was traveled over by horse cars, and the first locomotive ran upon it only thirty-five years ago. It was built in 1829 ; now the earnings of the road are over a million and a half dollars per annum."

Jonathan said nothing, but gave a little gasp of surprise.

" At Pier No. 2, is one of the Boston lines ; Pier No. 3 boats leave for Long Branch and Port Monmouth, and the splendid steamers belonging to the Savannah line start from Pier No. 4."

" What strange looking vessel is that?"

" That is the Bethel ship, used as a church for seamen. At Pier No. 11 are the steamers for Wilmington, Delaware, and at

Pier No. 13 are the boats for Savannah, New Orleans and New-bern. The boats for Savannah belong to the far-famed Empire side-wheel line, and leave every Saturday promptly at 3 o'clock, and run in connection with railroads throughout Georgia and Florida. For excellent accommodation for passengers, this line compares favorably with any. Messrs. Garrison & Allen, 5 Bowling Green, are the agents. Here are steamer upon steamers, from one to five thousand tons, clustering around the docks like boys hovering around a sugar barrel."

" A perfect forest of masts I do declare," chimed in Jonathan.

" Here, at the foot of Cortland street," I continued, " is the Jersey City Ferry, also connecting with the Erie Railroad, New Jersey Railroad, Northern Railroad of New Jersey, and the Morris and Essex Railroad."

" How large a population has Jersey City ? "

" About fifty thousand, and it is estimated that twenty-five thousand people, and two thousand vehicles cross this ferry daily."

" Goodness gracious! half of the inhabitants. How many boats are needed for so many passengers ? "

" Seven boats do it all, the largest of which is eight hundred tons."

" Rather a good size for a ferry boat."

" Yes, indeed."

. ' Does the ferry belong to the city ? " .

" No, to a company who pay to the city $5,000 for the privilege of carrying passengers across the river at three cents per head."

" A profitable speculation I should judge."

" Here, at Pier No. 19, is Washington Market, extending northerly to Pier No. 26. It was in old times called Bear Market, for, in those days, all the bear meat that came to the city was sold here. Piers 19 and 20 are crowded with propellers and canal boats ladened with produce of every kind to feed the hungry of the city."

Passing through Washington Market, we soon came to the first slip of the Hoboken Ferry, at the foot of Barclay street.

"Across this ferry is Hoboken, a great resort for rurally-disposed people. Its great charm are the Elysian Fields, which are much resorted to on Sundays by our German citizens who seek recreation and lager amid the sylvan groves of this far-famed place."

"The traffic does not seem so great here as at the Jersey City Ferry."

"It is not, but the proprietors do a pretty good business, notwithstanding. There are three ferries in all to Hoboken, for which the city receives $1,050 per year."

"Not an overwhelming sum for such privileges."

"The traffic, however, is rapidly increasing, and will no doubt continue so to do, for this reason, the North German Lloyds steamers for Bremen, *via* Southampton, sail from the pier at the foot of Third street, Hoboken, and the passengers for those vessels necessarily have to cross this ferry."

"Ah, I see."

"These vessels carry the United States mail, and are considered admirable sea going boats."

"They carry passengers of course?"

"Oh, yes, cabin, second cabin and steerage. for whom ample accommodations are provided."

"Now we have arrived at the wharf of the Erie Railroad Company. It is the great route to the West, and the most stupendous work of private enterprise ever executed in this country."

"You don't tell me!"

"Yes, it cost thirty millions of dollars, and is an enterprise, though it is not so profitable as it might be, that reflects great credit on the enterprise of New Yorkers."

"I guess I will return home by this route," said Jonathan.

"You could not do better, for since the great 'cut-off' has been completed, it is one of the most comfortable roads to travel on to the West."

"I will certainly go by this road," said Jonathan decidedly.

"At Salamanca, the Erie connects with the Atlantic and Great Western railway, thus enabling a person to travel all the way to Dayton, Ohio, on a broad guage track."

"That must not be forgotten," and Jonathan made an entry of the fact in his note book.

"Here, at Pier No. 33, the steamer Matteawan leaves daily at 3 p. m. for Middletown Point ; it is also the dock for the outside freight line to Philadelphia. At Piers 37 and 38 the ice ladened boats discharge their cargoes, here also is the wharf of the Delaware and Hudson Canal Company, who bring to this city over two hundred thousand tons of coal a year, nearly fifty thousand tons of which are landed at this wharf."

Jonathan only lifted up his hands in wonderment.

"At this wharf is the dumping ground for the manure and garbage collected in the streets ; usually there are about 1,200 loads dumped weekly, but in the spring when the accumulated filth of winter is collected, it frequently runs up to 2,000."

"Is this the only dumping place in the city ?"

"Dear me, no. There are several much larger on the East side of the city; the total amount dumped weekly is about 17,000 loads, which, in the spring, has been known to increase to as many as 40,000 loads."

"It appears to me that New York must be a very dirty place."

"Pier No. 41 is the landing place of the Albany boats. They are magnificent boats, and may well be called floating palaces. If you wish to see life and activity you should visit this dock a few minutes before 6 a. m. and 6 p. m.

"Is that the time the boats leave ?"

"It is. And if you never witnessed a scene of confusion, you will witness one then. Such hurrying, such shouting, a stranger would think they would never be ready to start at the appointed time. Heaps of freight upon the dock, and on board the boat. Deck hands busy wheeling it on board, while the ever-busy freight master stands, book in hand, tallying each package. Passengers arriving in carriages and on foot ; the baggage master surrounded by a sea of trunks, checking the same. The boat itself shrieking like a monster in pain, all, all combined to make a scene of confusion impossible to describe."

"I should like to witness it."

"So you ought ; but the months of July and August, when the people are rushing out of town to Niagara, Saratoga,

Canada, or any other place their fancies may dictate, is the time to see it at the height of its glory.''

"Just my luck," said Jonathan with a sigh, "I cannot be here those months.''

"At the foot of Canal street, is the second landing of the Hoboken Ferry; also the docks known as Pier No. 42, formerly occupied by the Collins line of steamers, now the starting place of the Pacific Mail Steamship Company's boats ''

"They go to California do they not?''

"Yes; they sail on the 1st, 11th and 21st of each month, except when either of those days fall on a Sunday, then they leave on the preceeding Saturday.''

"I have often thought I should like to go to California.''

"Well then, Jonathan, if you do make up your mind to go, you cannot do better than take your passage by this line. It is wonderfully well conducted, and every thing that can be done, is done by this Company for the comfort and accommodation of passengers.''

"How long does it take to go to California?''

"The average time is about twenty-two days; but it has been done by a steamer of this company—the *Arizona*, I believe—in eighteen days, twelve hours, that being the quickest time on record.''

"I have never been on board a large vessel, but I should much like to.''

"Then your wish shall be gratified.''

As good fortune would have it, the *Arizona* was lying at the dock, taking in cargo; so, obtaining permission to go on board, we at once set to work to examine the ship. Jonathan was much struck with her noble proportions—it was a revelation to him—and he babbled, delightedly, about all he saw.

The neatness and cleanliness of the state rooms were to him a theme of general laudation, while the cabin, with its elegance and beauty of fitting up, was fit for the abode of a prince.

With much reluctance, Jonathan left, and we wend. d our way past Clinton Market, and the piers opposite, at which a vast number of oyster boats were lying. Pointing these out to my companion, I told him that a large number of our oysters were landed at those docks, and that it was not an unusual thing, for 40,000 bushels to be sold there in one week.

"At pier No. 44, are the Inman line of steamships   They sail, semi-weekly, for Liverpool, calling at Queenstown."

"John," said Jonathan, suddenly stopping me, "I don't feel well."

"Not well ; what's the matter?"

"I don't know, but I think a little Bourbon would put me to rights."

We imbibed.

"Did you suffer any pain?"   I asked.

"No, I can't say I did, but I thought 'prevention was better than cure' any day."

I laughed, and thought any excuse better than none.

"Here, at Pier No. 47, is another steamship line to Europe. It is the National Steam Navigation Company's docks, and their vessels sail weekly for Queenstown and Liverpool."

"What a number of vessels sail for Great Britain."

"Yes, but our commercial relations are so great with that country, that there are none too many."

"I presume not."

"This," I continued, "is the cheapest line to Europe, as the cabin passage is only ninety dollars, and the steerage thirty, payable in currency."

"This certainly is cheap."

"It is. If you wanted to bring a poor friend out from Liverpool or Queenstown, you could do so by sending him a passage ticket, which would cost forty dollars."

"I thought you said thirty dollars, just now."

"So I did ; but the passage out takes longer, so the charge is higher."

"Ah, I understand."

At the foot of Christopher street is the third slip of the Hoboken Ferry, on either side of which are huge piles of lumber, towering upward toward the skies

"From here," I informed Jonathan, "the greater portion of our poorer class of citizens obtain their kindling wood "

"They get it here, then carry it home, and chop it up."

"It is sawed and split by steam, then done up into small bundles by boys, and sold to grocery store keepers for 1½ cents, and by them retailed for 2½ cents per bundle."

Jonathan's attention was now attracted by a huge floating box, that lay upon the water, having upon its deck a house, from which towered a gigantic mast, rigged with cross beams and pulleys. So he wished to know what it was.

"That is a derrick—Bishop's derrick, as it is generally called. It is used for raising sunken steamers, ships, and, in fact, all classes of vessels that may have foundered."

"Do you mean to tell me that that thing can raise a vessel from the bottom of the river?"

"I do indeed. With five men and one horse that arrangement has raised a boat with 300 tons of coal on board."

"Astonishing! I never would have believed it."

"This is done more by the lifting force of the boat itself, than by the power on board."

"How do you mean?"

"The boat being seventy-six feet square and twelve feet deep, it is only necessary to make her fast to a sunken boat at low tide, which, at high tide, will raise it six feet off the bottom."

"I see; the buoyancy of the derick doing this."

"Just so. It is then towed in nearer shore; at the next tide the process is repeated, until at last she is raised high enough to be pumped out."

"Well," said Jonathan taking off his hat and running his fingers through his hair, "we are a great people."

"Here," said I, when we had reached the foot of Fifteenth street, "is the crossing of the American Telegraph Company. The cable is three times as thick as the Atlantic Telegraph cable, and runs from here on the bed of the river to Brimstone Point in the Elysian Fields, Hoboken."

"Thence, I presume, all over the continent of America."

"Very nearly."

We were now at the foot of Eighteenth street, where a portion of the gas of the Manhattan Gas Company is made. It is the largest company in the city, and have another station for the manufacture of gas at the foot of Fourteenth street, East

River, and another at the foot of Sixty-fifth street, North River.

"Is this the only gas company in New York?"

"No, there is another one, which we will speak of anon. This company furnishes light to certainly not less than 350,-000 people, think of that, Jonathan."

"I do, and think it a most startling fact."

"In one year," I continued, "this company consumes a hundred thousand tons of coal, and sixty thousand bushels of lime, from which they make a thousand million cubic feet of gas."

Jonathan gave a little whistle of surprise.

"To do this fifteen hundred men are employed."

"They must have a vast quantity of piping laid throughout the city," Griggs remarked.

"Altogether about 230 miles of cast-iron main laid throughout the streets. But that will not so much surprise you when I tell you that the Manhattan Company light the whole of this great city from the north side of Grand street to the south side of Seventy-ninth street."

Still, steadily onward we progressed northward. Past swill-fed cow stables, that sickened us to look upon the forlorn, wretched, diseased animals therein confined ; by distilleries and slaughter-houses, making the air pregnant with poisonous vapors ; by sugar refineries, and pork packing establishments, with such facilities for the transaction of business, that hogs are killed, scalded, scraped, dressed, and ready for cooking, be· fore they know what has actually happened them.

Past great clipper ships that are being loaded and unloaded by steam ; past tow-boats ladened with the cereals of the West, the coal of Pennsylvania, and the thousand products of a thousand places ; past ships, and sloops and schooners that have brought the products of nearly every clime to our shores, and that are bound to a thousand different places ladened with the results of American industry and skill.

As we neared Thirty-fourth street I noticed that Jonathan gave three or four suggestive and unsatisfactory sniffs, finally pulling his handkerchief from his pocket, and applying it to his nose.

"What is the matter?" I asked.

"Do you not perceive a most disagreeable and offensive smell?"

"I do, but that is not to be wondered at, for at this pier is the offal boat."

"The offal boat!"

"Yes, the boat that receives the animal dead of the city, and the refuse of slaughter-houses. If your olfactories are not too sensitive we will go upon the dock and take a nearer view."

"The odor is not pleasant to my nostrils, but in the search for information I am prepared to suffer."

So upon the pier we went, and saw a small sloop lying there piled high with the carcases of horses, pigs, cows, dogs and cats, in every stage of decomposition. Besides these, a number of tubs and barrels filled with blood and entrails, stood about.

"How are these animals collected?"   .

"Whenever one dies, notice must immediately be given at the nearest station-house, or at the office of the City Inspector. The contractor then sends one of his carts—of which there are ten constantly employed—and the funeral takes place with neatness and dispatch."

"A terribly disagreeable business."

"The offal and blood from the slaughter-houses, the butchers are compelled by law to deliver themselves."

"And quite right and proper."

"The whole of this is done under the auspices of the Bureau of Sanitary Inspection, who, among other things, watch that the denizens of New York do not have unhealthy food sold to them."

"You do not mean to tell me," said Jonathan horrified, "that men sell food knowing it to be bad."

"We will give them the benefit of the doubt, and presume they are ignorant of it, but the officers of the Sanitary Inspection can detect it at once, and in one week condemned as unfit for human food, 1,236 pounds of beef; 495 pounds of veal ; 2,900 pounds of fish ; 350 pounds of poultry ; 3,580 pounds of other meats, and sixteen hogs."

"What an immense quantity!"

"But for this Bureau all this would have found its way down the throats of our hungry citizens, and engendered no end of sickness."

"Where is all this abomination carried to?"

"Up the river to a bone boiling establishment, where it is quickly converted into various articles much more useful."

"Let us go; I feel sick and faint."

"Now," said I, "as there is nothing more of any very great interest to be seen this side, we will cross over and and take a glimpse at the East River side.".

As we trudged along we talked of the commercial importance of New York, and the marvellous increase of her commerce, which has no parallel in history.

"In 1701," I informed Jonathan, "the mercantile marine of this city consisted of seventy-four vessels, seven of which were ships."

"Only seven ships!"

"Now the tonnage of the port of New York is nearly a million and a half tons, one-fifth of the entire United States."

"Immense, immense!" was all that Jonathan said.

"Here, at the foot of Thirty-fourth street, East River, is the ferry to Hunter's-Point, Long Island; at the foot of Twenty-third street is another ferry to Greenpoint."

"Apparently the means of egress from New York to the suburbs are ample."

"Yes, but not too many for our rapidly increasing growth. Here, also, is the other gas company I told you of—the New York. It is not so large as the Manhattan, their customers all being below Grand street."

"How many miles of main have they laid?"

About one hundred and thirty, they manufacture about six hundred millions cubic feet of gas per annum, and give employment to five hundred and thirty-five men."

"Here are the Novelty Iron Works, where the clang and clash of the hammer is never still, and the air is dark with the dust and labor of a thousand men."

"What! where they make the engines for ocean steamers?"

"The same ; and as we walk along, I will endeavor to give you some little description of the work."

"Pray commence."

"The entrance to the Novelty Works is by a great gateway, through which the visitor, on approaching it, will very probably see an enormous truck, or car, issuing, drawn by a long team of horses, and bearing some ponderous piece of machinery, suspended beneath it, by means of levers and chains. On the right of the entrance gate is the porter's lodge, with entrances from it to the offices. Beyond the entrance, and just within the inclosure, may be seen a great crane, used for receiving or delivering the vast masses of metal, the shafts, the cylinders, the boilers, the vacuum pans, and other ponderous formations, which are continually coming and going to and from the yard. Beyond the crane is seen the bell by which the hours of work are regulated."

"Which is, no doubt, heard with pleasure when it rings for dinner hour."

"On the right of the entrance is the porter's lodge ; beyond it, in the yard, stands the crane. Turning to the left, just beyond the crane, the visitor enters the iron foundry, a spacious inclosure, with ovens and furnaces along the sides, and enormous cranes swinging in various directions in the centre. These cranes are for hoisting the heavy castings out of the pits in which they are formed."

"And what are these ?"

"Those are ovens for drying the moulds. Turning to the right from the foundry, and passing down through the yard, the visitor finds himself in the midst of a complicated maze of buildings, which extend, in long ranges, toward the water, with lanes and passages between them, like the streets of a town. In these passages companies of workmen are seen, some going to and fro, drawing heavy masses of machinery upon iron trucks ; others employed in hoisting some ponderous cylinder or shaft by a crane, or stacking pigs of iron in great heaps, to be ready for the furnaces, which are roaring near, as if eager to devour them. And all the time there issues from the open doors of the great boiler-shops and forging-shops below, an incessant clangor, produced by the blows of the sledges upon the rivets of the boilers, or of the trip-hammers at the forges.

The motive power by which all the machinery of the establishment is driven, is furnished by a stationary engine, in the very centre of the works. It stands between two of the principal shops. On the right is seen the boiler, and on the left, the engine.

"This central engine, since it carries all the machinery of the works, by means of which everything is formed and fashioned, is the life and soul of the establishment—the *mother*, in fact, of all the monsters which issue from it; and it is impossible to look upon her, as she toils on industriously in her daily duty, and think of her Titanic progeny, scattered now over every ocean on the globe, without a certain feeling of respect, and even of admiration

"The number of men employed at the Novelty Works, is from one thousand to twelve hundred. These are all *men*, in the full vigor of life. If, now, we add to this number a proper estimate for the families of these men, and for the mechanics and artizans who supply their daily wants, all of whom reside in the streets surrounding the works, we shall find that the establishment represents, at a moderate calculation, a population of *ten thousand souls.*

"The proper regulation of the labors of so large a body of workmen as are employed in such an establishment, requires, of course, much system in the general arrangements, and very constant and careful supervision on the part of those intrusted with the charge of the various divisions of the work. The establishment forms, in fact, a regularly organized community, having, like any state or kingdom, its gradations of rank, its established usages, its written laws, its police, its finance. its records, its rewards, and its penalties."

As we passed on we saw the great skeletons of ships, gaunt and vast, lying upon the stocks. Hundreds of men were at work upon them, and the bustling activity, and the noisy hum of labor were pleasing to the sight and ear.

"John," said Jonathan, "I have never visited a ship-yard, and I should like to do so very much."

"Then you shall do so now, more especially as we are in the vicinity of the representative ship builder's yard of America."

"Indeed, then I am fortunate."

"I mean the ship-yard, at the foot of Sixth street, of Mr. William H. Webb, a builder who has constructed more ships than any other man in America."

"How many has he built altogether?"

"One hundred and twenty-nine vessels in his own yard, and a large number in other yards, making, as I have just now said, an aggregate of tonnage larger than any other American ship-builder."

"That is something to say, for ships go much toward making a country prosperous."

"His latest triumph in the way of marine architecture is the United States steam ram *Dunderberg*, launched on Saturday morning, July 22, 1865."

"I have read of her in the newspapers, and from all accounts she must be a wonderful vessel."

"She is an iron-clad frigate ram, of seven thousand tons displacement, five thousand tons registered tonnage, and of very peculiar construction. She is the most powerful and formidable vessel of her kind afloat, and the famous iron-clads of France or England cannot begin to compare with her."

"If England does not look out she will lose the supremacy of the seas."

"If she has not already done so ; and how has she done so ? I will tell you. By the skill, enterprise and energy of such men as Mr. Webb, of whom Americans are justly proud."

"How many guns will the *Dunderberg* carry?"

"Her armament will consist of four 15-inch Rodman's, and from twelve to fourteen 11-inch Dahlgreen guns."

"Goodness gracious ! sufficient to sink any ordinary ship in a few seconds."

"And that is what she is made for. Her dimensions are as follows : length, 380 feet 4 inches; beam, 72 feet 10 inches; height of casemate inside, 7 feet 9 inches ; length of ram-bow, 50 feet, and the iron armor upon her weighs 1,000 tons."

"She must be of immense draft."

"No, not so great as one would suppose, drawing, when ready for sea, only 21 feet. She has six main, and two donkey boilers. The engines are horizontal, back-action, condensing, with two 100-inch cylinders, and 45-inch stroke of piston.

Steamship "Constitution," built for the Pacific M. S. Co., launched by Wm. H. Webb, 1860.

The propeller is 31 feet in diameter. and has a varying pitch of from 27 to 30 feet, and weighs 34,580 pounds. Her coal-bunkers will accommodate 1,000 tons of coal, sufficient for 10 to 15 days steaming."

By this time we had reached the yard, and Jonathan watched with eager curiosity, the busy workmen, active as so many beavers, engaged upon the construction of a ship that, with ribs all bare and bleak, lay upon the stocks.

"If you like," I said to Jonathan, "I will give you a short sketch of Mr. Webb's most successful career."

"Nothing I should like better," he replied.

So, seating ourselves upon a heavy beam of timber, I commenced :

"William H. Webb, the eminent American ship-builder, was born in the city of New York, June 19, 1816. The family came from Connecticut, but was of English extraction. His father was the senior member of the firm of Webb & Allen, ship-builders in New York, and William, who had served his time with them at his father's dock, soon after became a partner in the business. This was in 1840, and this is the same ship-yard."

"Then Mr. Webb has been twenty-six years in business?"

" Yes. Three years later, Mr. Allen retired with a fortune, leaving the business entirely in Mr. Webb's hands. Having a great ambition to build a new vessel, in 1851 he applied to the proper officials of the American, French and Russian Governments, for a contract to build a frigate, but without success. During the next year he dispatched a special agent to St. Petersburg to press the matter there ; later, he sent a second agent, and at length, notwithstanding a great pressure of business at home, went himself to the Russian capital."

" A true American. The more difficulties the more determined to overcome them."

" At last, after about two months of hard work, he had made so favorable an impression on the Grand Duke (Constantine) that the latter obtained from the Emperor Nicholas an order for Webb to build in New York for the Russian Government, one line of-battle ship of ninety guns, and for its delivery at Cronstadt, with a large quantity of ship timber."

"Go on," commanded Jonathan somewhat excitedly " I am becoming quite interested."

" He returned to America, and preparations for the building of the ship were commenced at Mr. Webb's yard, but delays occurred by reason of the want of definite instructions on the part of the Russian naval officers sent out to superintend the work, and subsequently on account of the war between Russia and the Allied Powers of France and England. At the close of the war, Mr. Webb was directed to go on and build a ship with a less number, but larger guns. The keel of the *General Admiral* was laid September 21, 1857, in the presence of a large concourse of people, including the Russian Minister, Baron de Stoekle, his suite, and various Russian naval officers. The launch took place exactly one year later, and the vessel was completed and sent to Russia in 1859. The *General Admiral* was of about six thousand tons burden, carrying seventy-two guns, and fully met the expectations of the Russian Government."

" Of course, that was to be expected."

" From 1861 to 1863, Mr. Webb was engaged in the construction of two iron-clad frigates of six thousand tons, for the

Italian Government. The work on these vessels was prosecuted during the calamitous rebellion without interruption, and the ships, on their delivery to the Italian Government, provoked the most unbounded admiration.''

Jonathan was about to interrupt me, but I silenced him with a motion of my hand, and continued.

" Mr. Webb is truly a representative American. His astonishing career, his bold claim, not only for superiority over native but foreign ship-builders, and his determination, at every hazard and every cost, to demonstrate all this to the world, have proved him largely animated by the soaring ambition common to his nation.''

'' That's so ''

" And now let us sum up what he has done for the naval architecture of the world. He built a vessel which is the pride of the Russian navy ; he has placed two splendid iron-clad frigates in the navy of Italy, and now he contributes a new marvel to the navy of his own proud country. He has been enabled to do this because he was one of the born geniuses of the land, and because he determined to make his talents a new source of American renown.''

"Such a man,'' exclaimed Jonathan enthusiastically, ''is part of the history of the country.''

I was of the same opinion.

"At Pier 54, is where all the Italian marble is landed that is brought into this port. Those great blocks you see before you are destined to grow into life under the chisel of American sculptors.''

" What! those unshapely blocks of stone to be converted into works of art, it seems almost incredible.''

'' But nevertheless it is true. And here are the dry or sectional docks, most important adjuncts to a mercantile marine, where damaged or leaky ships are taken and repaired. There are two companies owning these docks, the 'Sectional Dock Company,' and the 'New York Balance Dock Company,' and have accommodation for five vessels.''

''What a number of men there are employed on a vessel ! ''

"Yes, it is no unusual sight to see two or three hundred men at once at work on a ship's bottom. The largest of these docks is 300 feet in length, and has a lifting power of 4,000 tons ; the power used is steam, and four men can lift the largest ship out of the water with the greatest ease—of course that is with the aid of the engine."

"You don't imagine," said Jonathan laughing, "that I supposed for a minute that four men could lift a ship without that aid ?"

"If," I continued, paying no heed to my companion's remark, "a vessel presents itself in a sinking condition, and the docks are full, a certificate to that effect will procure her admission to the United States sectional dock, at the Navy-Yard, Brooklyn, but not otherwise."

"What do they charge for hoisting out a vessel?"

"Twenty-five cents per ton for sailing vessels and fifty cents for steamers. At Pier 89 are the 'Hydrostatic Lifting Docks ;' pier No. 34 is the Catharine Ferry to Brooklyn, and pier No. 33 is where the oysters come in by the hundreds of tons."

We walked on.

"Pier No. 32 is another ferry to Hunter's Point; pier 29 another ferry to Williamsburg and Bridge street, Brooklyn. And here, at the foot of Beekman street, was started the first ferry to Brooklyn, in 1642. From that time the Brooklyn ferry became an established fact, and was removed to Fulton street some thirty or forty years ago."

"John," said Jonathan, looking up into my face, "I think an oyster would do me good."

" And I am also under the impression that a good roast or a stew would do me good. More especially as we are at Fulton Market, and it is only here that oysters can be obtained."

"Why, John, how you talk ! I am sure I have seen in the course of our walks no end of oyster saloons !"

"So you have ; but what I have spoken I have said advisedly, there is no place to get oysters in New York save Fulton Market."

"I did not know," remarked Jonathan, slyly, "that Fulton was an oyster market."

"Neither is it, in the strict sense of the term, but I allude · more particularly to the stand; or, more properly speaking to the Oyster Saloon of Messrs. Dorlan & Shaffer, situated at the south-eastern portion of the market.'

"Messrs. Dorlan & Shaffer," said Jonathan, inquiringly, "who are they?"

· "My dear fellow," I replied, somewhat sternly, "never ask that question again. Not to know them, is to argue yourself unknown."

Jonathan faltered out something about excusing him.

"They are," I continued, "one of the institutions of New York, and New York cannot be accounted seen unless a visit is paid to them."

"Then, how fortunate I suggested oysters."

I allowed Jonathan to take the praise to himself; but, if the truth was told, I was about doing the same myself.

"At my house," I went on, "since you have been staying with me, you have eaten oysters in nearly every style, and considered my stews as near perfection as possible"

"So I did, so I did;" and Jonathan smacked his lips at the recollection.

"They were nothing of the kind. Good, I admit; but as to being perfection! Nonsense!"

This cost me a hard struggle to admit; for, be it known, if there is one thing I pride myself on more than another, it is my stews.

"If any boay else had said that, John, I think I should have quarrelled with him."

"I don't know how it is, or why it should be," I resumed, "but what I am about to state will, I presume, be indorsed by all New Yorkers, or, indeed, I might say, by all oyster-eaters that ever visited this city."

"And that is?"

"It is impossible to get a roast, a stew, or a fry in your own house in the same manner you do at Dorlan and Shaffer's. Whether it is in the style of cooking, or what, I cannot tell, but certain it is, the fact stands as I have related."

"You know 'the proof of the pudding is in the eating,' so I will decide by-an'-by."

By this time we had reached the saloon, and my friend Jonathan was at once struck with the extreme neatness and capaciousness. At least, capacious for a stand in Fulton Market, for one hundred persons can be seated and served with crustacean delicacies at one and the same time.

We commenced on a stew, accompanied by a "toby" of ale. Our order was taken by a neat, active attendant, attired in a blue checked apron and sleeves, who, apparently, before we could say "Jack Robinson"—supposing we had wished to utter that gentleman's name—placed the desired articles before us.

Jonathan was astonished at the celerity with which our wishes were executed, and strongly asseverated it was like magic.

"Quickness is a necessity here," I remarked; "if the orders were not served expeditiously, one half of their customers could not be supplied."

"That I believe, judging from the people who are now present appeasing their gastronomic propensities with bivalves."

"Why, between the hours of six and twelve, P. M., no less than between three and four hundred ladies have been known to visit here, and partake of oysters, in one form or another. Of course, these were attended by cavaliers, swelling the number to no doubt, nearly a thousand."

"From such a business their receipts must be enormous."

"They are; on an average nearly fifteen hundred dollars being taken daily."

"You surprise me. Shall we try a roast?"

I acquiesced.

Some of the most noted people of New York and Brooklyn come here for oysters. Lawyers, politicians, literary men, editors, divines, and merchants, all, all visit this establishment, and indulge in their fondness for this delightful shellfish." And, as I spoke, I poised a beauty on the end of my fork, previous to swallowing it.

"Are there any celebrities here now?" queried Jonathan, in an audible whisper.

"Hush! not so loud. I will look in a minute."

In less than the specified time, I cast my eyes around the room, and espied several notables.

"Do you see that pleasant-faced, stoutly built gentleman, seated three tables from us?"

"That one with rather long hair? Yes."

"Well, he is the most popular preacher in Brooklyn, likewise the editor of one of the leading religious journals of the city."

"You don't mean that's—"

"Don't speak so loud ; everybody will hear you."

Jonathan lowered his voice, and whispered across the table, the name of one of our most famous divines.

"The same."

"What!" exclaimed Jonathan, surprised; "he come here?"

"And why not? Gentlemen of his cloth must eat as well as you and me, and everything here is as quiet and as well conducted as at any hotel in the land."

"That's so. I spoke without thinking."

"That lady there, seated at the table just opposite ours, is one of the most popular writers of the day, a regular contributor to Bonner's *Ledger*, and the authoress of several popular works, from the sale of which she has made a very comfortable fortune."

Jonathan gave a side-glance at the lady indicated.

"The gentleman with her, is her husband, he also is a literary man, a historian, and his lives of Aaron Burr, General Jackson and Horace Greeley are among the standard books of the English language."

A number of other notable people were present whom I pointed out for Jonathan's delectation.

By way of variety, Jonathan now proposed a fry, but to this I turned a deaf ear ; seeing he was disappointed at my refusal I insisted upon his taking one, which he did.

Everything must have an end, even an oyster meal, so Jonathan at last declared he was finished and had enjoyed himself exceedingly.

Before leaving Jonathan turned and took a last fond look and wiped away—not exactly a tear—but the crumbs from his mouth, and expressed, as his opinion, that Dorlan & Shaffer did a large business.

"They do. Taking their wholesale and retail business together none larger ; their trade extends all over the Continent of America, and they are constantly shipping to every State and Territory in the Union cans and barrels of oysters."

"Indeed, before leaving I must get them to send a few cans on to my place."

"It is generally supposed," I continued, "that no oysters fit to eat can be procured during the months of July and August ; this is a mistake."

"A mistake. Do not oysters spawn during the summer months ?"

"Yes. But the oysters that are eaten during the months I have mentioned are brought from Virginia, replanted in Prince's Bay, and dredged for when wanted."

"Do not Virginia oysters spawn at the same time as other oysters?"

"Oh, yes. What I meant was, by removing them the spawn is destroyed."

"Ah, I see."

By this time we had left the market ; looking up Fulton street I pointed out to Jonathan the old United States Hotel, at the corner of Water and the above mentioned street.

"That hotel was a famous one in its day. It was the resort and home of marine captains, and seafaring men. Now it is no longer used as a hotel, but is let out for offices."

"Changes are taking place every day," said Jonathan somewhat sententiously.

"That's true. In the building, at 196 Water street, is the United States lunch-room, decidedly the best at this portion of the city, as the merchants and clerks in this vicinity amply testify, by their visiting it to satisfy the cravings of the inner man."

"A large rush of customers is a sure criterion that the edibles and drinkables of such an establishment are excellent."

"That's so. The proprietors are Messrs. Andrews & Terry, gentlemen of large experience as caterers for the appetite of the public."

U. S. LUNCH ROOMS, 196 Water Street.

"John," said Jonathan solemnly, placing his hand on the lower button of his waistcoat, "I think those oysters want a corrective."

"A corrective!"

"Yes. I always use Bourbon, what do you take?"

I could not help smiling, as I replied that Bourbon was also my favorite medicine.

"And," I continued, "as we are now at 91 South street, kept by Messrs. Farrar & Lyon, we will just drop in and try some of their superb old Kentucky whisky."

"Well," said Jonathan when he had tasted it, "this is really excellent; some of the right sort, and no mistake."

"You are right, it is. The firm of Farrar & Lyon have been in business for over half a century, consequently they have long experience, and have greater facilities for the transaction of business, and obtaining pure and genuine articles than almost any other house can boast of."

"Judging from the sample I have just swallowed, I believe it."

"Before leaving, we will just take a stroll through their vaults and store rooms;" so saying I led the way to escort Jonathan through the building.

We saw thousands upon thousands of cigars, piled box upon box, reaching from the floor to the ceiling; barrels upon barrels of liquors and the most precious wines, and innumerable demijohns upon the floors, on shelves, and suspended on hooks from the rafters above.

"What an immense stock!" ejaculated Jonathan.

"One of the largest in the trade. Besides the supply you see here, this house always has a large quantity of wines, liquors and cigars stored away in bond, so it is safe to calculate the stock twice as large as that which meets the eye on a tour through the premises."

"It must take a large capital to conduct such a business."

"Over a quarter of a million dollars, I believe, is the capital used by this house. You were talking just now of the excellence of the Bourbon?"

"I was John, and it is good."

"Then this may be a consolation to you; wherever you go

throughout the Continent of America, you will always be enabled to procure some of it."

" By carrying it with me, I presume you mean."

" No, I mean that Messrs. Farrar & Lyon have customers in nearly every town and city in the Union, so you see, with very little difficulty you can procure some of their Bourbon."

" I do see."

" Or," I continued, warming with my theme, " if business or chance should have you visit foreign lands, you can still obtain a " smile " from the cellars of those gentlemen."

" How so ? "

" There is hardly an American vessel, either sailing or steam, that leaves this port that does not get her supply of wines, liquors and cigars from this house."

" Ah, I see ; that information is worth mentally noting."

We now resumed our walk along the wharves.

" Pier No. 26 is now occupied by the Peck Slip Ferry Company to Williamsburg. This Company pays to the city the sum of $21,000 per annum for the privilege of ferrying passengers across at this point."

" A good round sum."

" Yes, but the Company make money out of it even at that. Piers No. 24 and 25 are the docks of the New Haven and Hartford steamboats. From Piers 20 to 21 is Burling Slip. Talking of Burling Slip reminds me ; if you ever become thirsty in this neighborhood drop in at No. 40½, the Ocean House, and my word for it, you will be thoroughly satisfied with what you obtain."

" Upon my word John, you know everything."

Paying no attention to Jonathan's interpolation, I continued.

" At the foot of Wall street is Pier No. 16. From here start the fast sailing Murray's Line of steamships for Savannah. The boats are the *Leo* and *Virgo*, both staunch sailing crafts, and fitted up with every convenience for the accommodation of passengers. They leave every Thursday at 3 o'clock P. M."

" Is this another market ? "

" Yes, the Franklin, formerly known as the Old Fly Market. It was the first market established in this city, though now it is not much used."

" What great ugly looking thing is that, moored off the pier?"

"That is the dredging machine."

"Used for dredging oysters?"

"Still harping on your oysters. No; it is commonly called a 'mud scow,' and is used for cleaning the docks of the accumulated mud and filth that is not worked off by the ebb and flow of the tide."

"Useful, but certainly not ornamental."

"At Pier No. 2 are the slips of the South and Hamilton Ferries to Brooklyn. On Pier No. 1 is the barge office, where inspectors of customs wait, when not on actual duty, to be assigned to incoming vessels so as to watch over the interests of Uncle Sam; on this pier is also the office of the Associated Press, and in the boat-house below, the Harbor Police keep their boats. Here is also the ferry to Staten Island."

"If I am not mistaken, this is the Battery, where we started from this morning?"

"It is."

"I thought so, and now John, as I am somewhat tired, let us get into an omnibus and ride to your residence."

"One moment; before we leave the wharves and shipping let me rectify an omission I made passing up along the docks of the North River."

"An omission! what was that?"

"Forgetting to point out to you 'The North American Lloyd' line of steamships that run from this port to Bremen."

"Is it such an excellent one?"

"Not only that, but it is the only purely American line that runs between here and Europe. All the mail steamships, for the past few years, to Europe, have been owned by foreign companies. Consequently, when we see an American company striving to break down this monopoly, we, as Americans, should give it our most cordial recognition.

"That's most emphatically so."

"The pier of this company is at No. 46 North River; office 45 Beaver street, and the steamers, carrying the United States' mail, leave bi-monthly for Bremen, touching at Cowes, where passengers for France and England are transhipped."

Having had my say, I hailed a passing stage, and getting into it, we were carried up Broadway towards home.

WALK THE SEVENTH.

CHURCHES.

It had been my intention on this, the seventh day of our peregrinations, to have taken Jonathan to some of our leading churches. But, upon examination, I found they were so numerous that it would be impossible to visit them all in one day. So 1 compromised the matter by giving Jonathan the following list, which is a correct one, of New York churches :

BAPTIST.

Abyssinian, 166 Waverly Place ; W. Spelman, Minister, 70 Grove street; Moses Wester, Sexton, at church.

Amity Street, 161 Fifth avenue ; R. Brownlow, Sexton, 17 Amity Place.

Antioch, 264 Bleecker street; John Q. Adams, Minister, 63 Morton street.

Berean, 85 Downing street ; John Dowling, Minister, 6 Ashland Place ; William Morgan, Sexton, 25 Bedford street.

Bethesda, Fifty-third street, near Seventh avenue; W. H. Pendleton, Minister ; Azariah Clark, Sexton.

Bethlehem, 395 West Forty-fifth street; Charles Gayer, Minister ; C. Gauger, Sexton, at church.

Bloomingdale, 220 West Forty second street; I. Westcott, Minister, 200 W. Forty-second street.

Calvary, 50 West Twenty-third street ; R. J. W. Buckland, Minister, 445 West Twenty-third street; Henry Estwick, Sexton, 1276 Broadway.

Cannon Street, Madison street, corner Governeur ; E. K. Fuller, Minister.

Ebenezer, 154 West Thirty-sixth street; James C. Gobel, Minister ; M. A. Quackenbush, Sexton, at church.

Fifth Avenue, near West Forty-sixth street ; Thomas Armitage, Minister, 850 Broome street.

Fifth Avenue, near West One Hundred and Twenty-sixth street ; Elijah Lucas, Minister, West One Hundred and Twenty-fifth street, corner Seventh avenue.

First, 354 Broome street ; Thomas D. Anderson, Minister, at church ; Joseph Young, Sexton, 357 Broome street.

First German, 19 Avenue A ; John Eschman, Minister, 19 Avenue A.

First Mariners', Oliver street, corner Henry street ; J. H. Hodge, Minister, Brooklyn ; John Davis, Sexton, 32 Henry street.

Free-Will Baptist, 74 West Seventeenth street.

Laight Street, corner Varick street ; Robert McGonegal, Minister, 16 Beach street ; Thomas Richards, Sexton, 2 Watts street.

Macdougal Street, 24 Macdougal street ; L. W. Olney, Minister ; D. Baschau, Sexton, 31 Cornelia street.

Madison Avenue, corner East Thirty-first street ; Henry G. Weston, Minister, 140 East Thirty-first street ; S. Douglass, Sexton, 461 Third avenue.

North, 126 Christopher street ; A. Cleghorn, Minister.

Pilgrim, West Thirty-third street, near Eighth avenue ; W. Clark, Sexton, 377 Ninth avenue.

Sixth Street, 211 Sixth street ; J. Senior, Sexton, 613 Fifth street.

Sixteenth Street, 257 West Sixteenth street ; W. S. Mikels, Minister, 174 West Seventeenth street ; James Carpenter, Sexton, 147 West Eighteenth street.

South, 147 West Twenty-fifth street ; H. W. Knapp, Minister ; J. Vanbrakle, Sexton, 335 Eighth avenue.

Stanton Street, 36 Stanton street ; T. C. Fisher, Sexton.

Tabernacle, 162 Second avenue ; J. R. Kendrick, Minister ; R. Brownlow, Sexton, 17 Amity Place.

Welsh, 141 Christie street ; Laban Lewis, Sexton, 141 Christie street.

Yorkville, East Eighty-third street, near Second avenue ; C. C. Norton, Minister, East Eighty-second street, near Third avenue ; G. Walters, Sexton, East Eightieth street, near Second avenue.

Zion (colored,) 155 Sullivan street ; J. R. Raymond, Minister ; A. Duncan, Sexton, 15 Laurens street.

CONGREGATIONAL.

Bethesda (colored,) 681 Sixth avenue; C. B. Ray, Minister, 81 West Thirty eight street; George Rogers, Sexton.

Church of the Puritans, Union Place, corner East Fifteenth street; G. B. Cheever, Minister; A. A. McGee, Sexton, 117 West Thirty-third street.

Tabernacle, Sixth avenue, corner West Thirty-fourth street; J. P. Thompson, Minister, 32 West Thirty-sixth street; Frederick S. Boyd, Sexton, 47 West Thirty-fifth street.

Welsh, 33 East Eleventh street; Evan Griffiths, Minister, 171 Eighth avenue.

St. John's Forty-first street, near Sixth avenue

DUTCH REFORMED.

Bloomingdale, Broadway, corner West Sixty-eighth street; Enoch Vanaken, Minister, 47 West Twenty-ninth street.

Collegiate, Lafayette Place, corner East Fourth street; North Dutch, William street, corner Fulton street; Fifth Avenue, corner West Twenty-ninth street; Lecture-room, West Forty-eighth street, near Fifth avenue; Thomas Dewitt, 123 Ninth street, T. E. Vermilye, 20 East Thirty-seventh street, T. W. Chambers, 70 West Thirty-sixth street, and J. T. Duryea, 26 West Thirty-sixth street, Ministers; Arch. C. Brady, 100 East Fourth street; James Dunshee, 22 King street, and W. J. Schoonmaker, 65 West Twenty-ninth street, Sextons.

Fourth German Mission, 112 West Twenty-ninth street; J. H. Oerter, Minister, 143 West Thirty-first street.

German Evangelical Mission, 141 East Houston street; Julius W. Geyer, Minister, 215 Forsyth street; William Roth Sexton, rear of church.

German Reformed Protestant, 129 Norfolk street; H. A. Friedel, 127 Norfolk street; Frederick Tromp, Sexton, at church.

Greenwich, 53 West Forty-sixth street; Thomas C. Strong, Minister.

Harlem, Third avenue, corner East One Hundred and Twenty first street; Jer. S. Lord, Minister, rear of church.

Manhattan, 71 Avenue B ; Ebenezer Wiggins, Minister, 408 Fifth street ; H. Miller, Sexton, 406 Fifth street.

Market Street, corner Henry street ; J. C. Dutcher, Minister, 235 Henry street ; T. P Rogers, Sexton, 238 Clinton street.

Mount Pleasant, 158 East Fiftieth street ; Isaac M. See, Minister, 151 East Fiftieth street.

North Dutch. (See Collegiate.)

North West, 145 West Twenty-third street ; H. D. Ganse, Minister, 358 West Twenty-second street ; W. Allason, Sexton, 102 West Twenty-fourth street.

Prospect Hill, Third avenue, near East Eighty-seventh street; D. McL. Quackenbush, Minister, East Eighty-sixth street, near Third avenue ; J. Chandler, Sexton, Third avenue, near East Eighty-fifth street.

South, Fifth avenue, corner West Twenty-first street ; E. P. Rogers, Minister, 5 East Thirty-first street ; J. Young, Sexton, 52 Third avenue.

Thirty-Fourth Street, 307 West Thirty-fourth street ; Peter Stryker, Minister, 205 West Thirty-first street ; John Cleverley, Sexton, 495 Eighth avenue.

Twenty-First Street, 47 West Twenty-first street ; A. R Thompson, Minister, 25 West Twenty-seventh street ; J. S. Brady, Sexton, 447 West Forty-fourth street.

Union, 25 Sixth avenue ; Isaac L. Hartley, Minister, 147 West Fifteenth street.

Washington Heights.

Washington Square, Washington Square, East corner Washington Place ; Mancius S. Hutton, Minister, 115 Ninth street ; Thomas Burton, Sexton, next to church.

FRIENDS.

East Fifteenth Street, corner of Rutherford Place ; William Barry, Janitor, at church.

East Twentieth Street, near Third avenue ; B. Barrington, Janitor.

West Twenty Seventh Street ; J. W. Onderdonk, 1,252 Broadway.

JEWISH SYNAGOGUES.

Adaareth El, East Twenty-ninth street, near Third avenue; Charles Musch, President, 114 Third avenue.

Adas Jeshurun, 65 West Thirty-fourth street; E. Schwab, President.

Ahawath Chesed, Avenue C, corner of East Fourth street; Ignatz Stein, President; D. Nessler, sexton, 41 Avenue C.

Anshi Bikur Cholim, Ridge street, corner of East Houston street; M. Westheimer, President.

Anshi Chesed, 146 Norfolk street; M. Schwab, President; A. Sternberg, Reader; Simon Hermann, sexton, 146 Norfolk street.

Beth Cholim, 138 West Twenty-eighth street; B. Nathan President.

Beth Joseph, 45 East Broadway; A. Alex..nder, President.

Beth El, 176 West Thirty-third street; Jacob Lewis, President; Jacob Bergmann, sexton, 171 West Thirty-third street.

Beth Hamidrash, 78 Allen street; B. Goldstein, President; A. Jacobs, sexton, 78 Allen street.

Beth Hamidrash Second, 157 Chatham street; Isadore Raphael, President.

Beth Israel Bikur Cholim, 56 Chrystie street; S. Kreuter, President; I. Bielefeld, sexton, 56 Chrystie street.

Bikur Cholim, U-Kadischa, 63 Chrystie street; —— Levy, President; J. Keiser, sexton.

Bnai Israel, 41 Stanton street; E. N. Ezekiels, President; K. Rose, sexton, 41 Stanton street.

Bnai Jeshurun, 145 West Thirty-fourth street; Israel J. Solomon, President; M. J. Raphall, Rabbi Preacher, 46 West Washington Place; J. Kramer, Minister, 174 West Thirty-third street; J. Joel, sexton, at the church.

Bnai Sholom, 127½ Columbia street; A. Bar, President, 405 East Houston street.

Mischkan Israel, Allen street, corner of Grand street.

Poel Zedeck, West Twenty-ninth street, corner of Eighth avenue; D. Kempner, President.

Rodeph Shalom, 8 Clinton street; S. Hyman, President; J. Kimmelstiel, sexton, at the church.

Shaarai Berocho, 275 Ninth street ; J. Abrahams, President ; S. Sachs, sexton, 121 First avenue.

Shaarai Rach Mim, 156 Attorney street ; N. Sonneberg, President, 115 Avenue C ; D. Frank, Reader ; D. Straus, sexton, 169 Second street.

Shaarai Tephila, 1,306 Broadway ; T. L. Solomons, President ; S. M. Isaacs, Minister, 145 West Forty-sixth street ; J. Bildersee, sexton, at the church.

Shaarai Zedek, 38 Henry street ; S. D. Moss, President.

Shaaer Hashamoin, 91 Rivington street ; H. Eckstein, President ; R. Lasker, Minister ; Isaac Fink, sexton, at the church.

Shearith Israel, West Nineteenth street near Fifth avenue ; I. Abecasis, President ; J. J. Lyons, Minister, 77 Seventh avenue ; S. Isaacs, sexton.

Temple, 84 East Twelfth street ; A. Michelbacher, President ; Samuel Adler, Rabbi, 124 East Thirty-first street ; A. Rubin, Reader ; S. Kakelcs, sexton, 324 Third avenue.

LUTHERAN

Lutheran, Avenue B, corner of Ninth street ; F. W. Foehlinger, Minister. 303 Ninth street.

St. James', 103 East Fifteenth street ; A. C. Wedekind, Minister ; P. Smith, sexton, 95 Macdougal street.

St. John's, 81 Christopher street ; A. H. M. Held, Minister, 290 Bleeker street ; Peter Asmussen, sexton, 343 Bleecker street.

St. Luke's 208 West Forty-third street ; G. W. Drees, Minister, 99 West Forty-first street ; J. Burckhardt, sexton, 447 Ninth avenue.

St. Marcus', 52 Sixth street ; H. Ragener, Minister, 138 Second street ; John Theisz, sexton, 238 Ninth street.

St. Matthew's, Walker street, corner of Cortlandt alley ; C. F. E. Stohlmann, Minister, 167 Mott street ; Charles F. Hobe, sexton.

St. Paul's 226 Sixth avenue ; F. W. Geissenhainer, Minister, 76 East Fourteenth street ; John Fackiner, sexton, 112 West Fifteenth street.

St. Peter's, 125 East Fiftieth street; C. Henicke, Minister, house next the church; C. Heckel, sexton, 218 East Fifty-second street.

Yorkville, East Eighty-seventh street, near Fourth avenue; G. J. Rentz, Minister, Fourth avenue, near East Eighty-ninth street.

METHODIST EPISCOPAL.

Presiding Elders: New York District, M. D. C. Crawford, 237 West Nineteenth street; New York East District, E. E. Griswold.

Alanson, 55 Norfolk street; parsonage, 155 Clinton street T. R. Ryers, sexton, 55 Norfolk street.

Allen Street, 126 Allen.street; parsonage, 128 Allen street; J. L. Kellogg, sexton, 61 First street.

Bedford Street, 28 Morton street; parsonage, 47 Morton street; Beckman Hill, East Fiftieth street, near Second avenue.

Bethel Ship, foot of Carlisle street; O. G. Hedstrom, minister Jersey City.

Central, 44 Seventh avenue; parsonage, 46 Seventh avenue; James Anderson, sexton, 370 Bleeker street.

Central Park Mission, Third avenue, corner of East Seventieth street.

Duane Street, 294 Hudson street.

Eighteenth Street, 193 West Eighteenth street; parsonage, 191 West Eighteenth street; J. B. Smith, sexton, 169 West Eighteenth street.

Fiftieth Street, Lexington avenue, corner East Fifty-second street; Parsonage. 114 East Fiftieth street; C. Stockinger, sexton. 773 Third avenue.

Fifty-third Street, 135 West Fifty-third street; parsonage, 137 West Fifty-third street.

Forsyth Street, 10 Forsyth street; parsonage, 12 Forsyth street; P. Beach, sexton, rear 11 Eldridge street.

Forty-third Street, 177 West Forty-third street; parsonage, 175 West Forty-third street; J. Lapthorn, sexton, 182½ West Forty-fourth street.

German, 252 Second street; parsonage, 256 Second street; J. Muck, sexton, 256 Second street.

German Mission, 222 West Fortieth street.

Greene Street, 59 Greene street ; parsonage, 57 Greene street.

Harlem, East One Hundred and Twenty-fifth street, near Third avenue ; parsonage, East One Hundred and Twenty-seventh street, near Third avenue ; W. H. Perine, sexton, 1,946 Third avenue.

Hedding, 170 East Seventeenth street; parsonage, 168 East Seventeenth street ; J. Barry, sexton, 426 Second avenue.

Jane Street, 13 Jane street ; parsonage, 11 Jane street.

Janes Mission, 461 West Forty-fourth street.

John Street, 44 John street ; Henry Davis, sexton, 453 Greenwich street.

Ladies' Home Mission, 61 Park street.

Rose-Hill, 125 East Twenty-seventh street ; parsonage, 123 East Twenty-seventh street.

St. Paul's Fourth avenue, corner of East Twenty-second street ; parsonage, 289 Fourth avenue ; T. H. Patterson, sexton, 64 East Twenty-fifth street.

Second Avenue, corner of East One Hundred and Nineteenth street.

Second Street, 276 Second street; parsonage, 280 Second street , Cornelius Waldron, sexton, 268 Second street.

Seventh Street, 24 Seventh street ; parsonage, 22 Seventh street ; E. Lewis, sexton, 50 Third avenue ; Mission, 306 East Fourth street.

Thirtieth Street, 207 West Thirtieth street ; parsonage, 203 West Thirtieth street.

Thirty-seventh Street, 129 East Thirty-seventh street ; parsonage, 183 East Thirty-seventh street ; James Mills, sexton, 483 Third avenue.

Trinity, 248 West Thirty-fourth street ; parsonage, 263 West Thirty-fourth street ; Thomas Haight, sexton, 148 West Thirty-third street.

Twenty-fourth Street, 251 West Twenty-fourth street ; parsonage, 272 West Twenty-fourth street.

Washington Square, 137 West Fourth street ; parsonage, 80 Macdougal street ; F. C. Senior, sexton, 84 Bedford street.

West Harlem, West One Hundred and Twenty-fifth street,

near Sixth avenue; Albert H. Wyatt, Minister, 33 East One Hundred and Twenty-ninth street.

Willet Street, 7 Willet street; parsonage, 5 Willet street; Alfred C. Vallotton, sexton, 14 Willet street.

Yorkville, East Eighty-sixth street, near Fourth avenue; parsonage, next to the church; J. Chapman, sexton, East Eighty-eighth street, near Fourth avenue.

AFRICAN METHODIST EPISCOPAL.

African Union, 161 West Fifteenth street; R. G. Wilson, Minister.

Bethel,·214 Sullivan street; R. P. Gibbs, Minister; J. Cooper, sexton, 215 Sullivan street.

Zion, 331 Bleecker street; S. Jones, Minister, 76 Sullivan street; John Darnel, sexton, 154 Sullivan street.

METHODIST PROTESTANT

First, 87 Attorney street; W. C. Clark, Minister, 7 Eldridge street; Thomas Brown, sexton, 192 Rivington street.

PRESBYTERIAN.

African Union (colored,) 157 West Twenty-eighth street; P. Hopkins, Minister.

Allen Street, 61 Allen street; William W. Newell, Minister, 66 Second avenue; J. T. Reed, sexton, 81 First street.

Brick, Fifth avenue, corner West Thirty-seventh street; Gardiner Spring, Minister, 13 West Thirty-seventh street; J. O. Murray Assistant; James S. Hull, sexton, 65 Second street.

Canal Street, 7 Green street; A. Carlyle, sexton.

Central, 400 Broome street; James B Dunn, Minister, 186 West Nineteenth street; P. Hickok, sexton.

Chelsea, 353 West Twenty-second street; E. D. Smith, Minister, 290 West Twenty-first street; William Stevenson, sexton 416 West Twenty-fifth street.

Covenant, Fourth avenue, corner East Thirty-fifth street, George L. Prentiss, Minister, 70 East Twenty-seventh street C. Cullen, sexton.

Church of the Covenant, (colored,) 231 West Sixteenth street ; H. M. Wilson, Minister, 26 Bible house.

Eighty-Fourth Street, near Bloomingdale road ; F. L. Patton.

Eleventh, East Fifty-fifth street, near Lexington avenue ; A. E. Kittredge, Minister, Lexington avenue, near East Fifty-fourth street ; E. Keeler, sexton, 157 East Fifty-eighth street.

Fifteenth Street, 71 East Fifteenth street ; Samuel D. Alexander, Minister, 90 East Twenty-second street.

Fifth Avenue, corner East Nineteenth street ; N. L. Rice, Minister, 30 West Eighteenth street ; William Culyer, sexton, 231 Thompson street.

First, Fifth avenue, corner West Eleventh street ; William M. Paxton, Minister ; Charles J. Day, sexton, 196 West Eighteenth street.

Forty-Second Street, 233 West Forty-second street ; W. A. Scott, Minister ; J. M. Vannett, sexton, 117 West Forty-first street.

Fourth Avenue, 286 Fourth avenue ; Howard Crosby, Minister.

Fourteenth Street, corner Second avenue ; L. M. Keeler, Sexton, 101 East Fourth street.

Fortieth Street, corner Lexington avenue ; Charles E. Hart, Minister, 48 West Thirty-sixth street.

French Evangelical, 9 University Place ; J. B. C. Beaubien, Minister, 62 West Fourth street.

German, 290 Madison street ; Fred. Steins, Minister, 288 Madison street ; Henry Oberback, sexton, 36 Montgomery street.

Grand Street, West Thirty-fourth street, near Broadway ; John Thompson, Minister, 307 West Twenty-fourth street ; R. Robertson, sexton.

Harlem, East One Hundred and Twenty-seventh street, near Third avenue ; Ezra H. Gillett, Minister, East One Hundred and Twenty-ninth street, near Fifth avenue.

Lexington Avenue, corner East Forty-sixth street ; Joseph Sanderson, Minister, rear of church ; R. McQuhae, sexton, 641 Third avenue.

Madison Square, Madison avenue, corner East Twenth-fourth

street ; William Adams, Minister, 8 East Twenty-fourth street ; James S. Huyler, sexton, 235 Sullivan street. Mission, 419 Third avenue ; C. H. Payson, Minister, 95 East Thirty-sixth street.

Manhattanville, West One Hundred and Twenty-sixth street, corner Ninth avenue ; E. P. Payson, Minister.

Mercer Street, near Waverly Place ; R. R. Booth, Minister, 77 Ninth street ; John Culyer, sexton, 231 Thompson street.

Mission, West Thirty-third street, corner Eighth avenue ; R. C. Shimeall, Minister, 371 West Thirty-fifth street.

Mission Chapel, 107 Seventh avenue ; Morse Rowell, Minister.

Mount Washington, near Kingsbridge ; R. W. Dickinson, Minister.

North, Ninth avenue, corner West Thirty-first street ; Thos. Street, Minister, 9 Lamartine Place ; Alfred W. Walker, sexton, 360 Ninth avenue.

Prince Street, corner Marion, (colored ;) J. S. Martin, Minister ; Thomas Jackson, sexton.

Rutgers Street, Madison avenue, corner East Twenty-ninth street ; J. M. Krebs, Minister, 88 East Thirty-ninth street ; J. P. Cantrell, sexton, 393 Fourth avenue.'

Scotch, 53 West Fourteenth street ; Joseph McElroy, Minister, 63 West Nineteenth street ; Charles A. Stuart, sexton, 126 West Thirteenth street.

Seventh, Broome street, corner Ridge street ; Thomas Ralston Smith, Minister, 23 Rutgers Place ; Andrew J. Case, sexton, 397 Grand street.

Spring Street, 246 Spring street ; J. D. Wilson, Minister, 137 West Thirteenth street ; J. Ford, sexton, 30 Vandam street.

Thirteenth Street, 115 West Thirteenth street ; S. D. Burchard, Minister, 45 Seventh avenue ; J. Hanna, sexton, 7 Seventh avenue.

Twenty-Eighth Street, 252 West Twenty-eighth street ; W. B. Sutherland, Minister ; Robert McHugh, sexton, at church.

Twenty-Third Street, 210 West Twenty-third street ; Fred. G. Clark, Minister, 201 West Twenty-third street ; F. P. Wood, sexton, 266 Eighth avenue.

University Place, corner Tenth street ; A. H. Kellogg, Minister ; N. Wilson, sexton, 16 Tenth street.

Washington Heights, Charles A. Stoldard, Minister.

West, West Forty-second street, near Fifth avenue ; Thomas S. Hastings, Minister, 81 West Forty-fifth street ; J. Main, sexton.

West Fiftieth, 166 West Fiftieth street, S. B. Bell, Minister.

Westminster, 151 West Twenty-second street ; Alexander B. Jack, Minister.

Yorkville, 147 East Eighty-sixth street; A. P. Botsford, Minister, 141 East Eighty-sixth street ; J, Martin, sexton, Third avenue, near East Eighty-fourth street.

UNITED PRESBYTERIAN.

Eleventh Street, 33 East Eleventh street ; J. A. McGill, Minister.

Jane Street, 41 Jane street ; John Brash, Minister, 202 West Twentieth street ; John Watson, sexton, 41 Jane street.

Seventh Avenue, 20 Seventh avenue ; James Harper, Minister ; Charles Ellis, sexton, at church.

Seventh, 434 West Forty-fourth street ; G. Cambell, Minister 435 West Forty-fourth street ; J. Whitehead, sexton, at church.

Third, 41 Charles street ; Hugh H. Blair, Minister, 34 Perry street ; Robert Carnes, sexton, rear 41 Charles street.

West Twenty-Fifth Street, 161 West Twenty-fifth street ; James Thompson, Minister, 241 West Twenty-second street ; W. Cochran, sexton, at church.

ASSOCIATE REFORMED PRESBYTERIAN.

Fourth, 157 Thompson street ; William Freeland, Minister, next to church ; Joseph Greer, sexton, at church.

REFORMED PRESBYTERIAN.

First, 123 West Twelfth street ; J. N. McLeod, Minister, 147 West Twenty-second street.

Second, Clinton Hall ; S. L. Finney, Minister, A. J. Park, sexton.

Second, 167 West Eleventh street ; Andrew Stevenson, Minister, 341 West Twelfth street ; Samuel G. Williams, sexton at church.

Third, 238 West Twenty-third street ; J. R. W. Sloane. Minister, 203 West Twenty-second street ; William Hill, sexton. 196 Seventh avenue.

Sullivan Street, 101 Sullivan street ; J. C. K. Milligan, Minister, 200 West Twentieth street ; Robert Milford, sexton, 101 Sullivan street.

PROTESTANT EPISCOPAL.

Rt. Rev. Horatio Potter, Bishop, 83 West Thirty-fourth street.

Advent, 725 Sixth avenue ; A. Bloomer Hart. Rector, 762 Broadway ; John Parkinson, sexton.

All Angels, West Eighty-first, corner Eleventh avenue ; C. E. Phelps, Rector, near the church.

All Saints, 286 Henry street; S. J. Corneille, Minister, 89 Governeur street ; A. W. Fraser, sexton, 19 Scammel street.

Annunciation, 110 West Fourteenth street ; S. Seabury, Rector, West Twentieth street, near Ninth avenue ; E. H. Cressy, Assistant, 44 Ninth street ; S. W. Gilham, sexton, 127 Sullivan street.

Ascension, Fifth avenue, corner Tenth street; John Cotton Smith, Rector, 61 Tenth street ; W. Donaldson, sexton.

Calvary, Fourth avenue, corner East Twenty-first street ; E. A. Washburn, Rector, 64 East Twenty-first street ; James Adair, sexton, 351 Fourth avenue. Mission, 133 East Twenty-third street ; W. D. Walker, Minister, 82 East Twenty-third street ; James Aikens, sexton, 401 Second avenue.

Chapel of the Holy Comforter, foot of Hubert street, North river ; H. F. Roberts, Minister ; Charles Hernberg, sexton.

Christ, Fifth avenue, corner of East Thirty-fifth street ; F. C. Ewer, Rector, 137 West Forty-second street ; G. Radan, sexton, 547 Sixth avenue. Mission, 176 West Eighteenth street ; Thomas Cook, Minister.

Du St. Esprit, 30 West Twenty-second street ; A. Verren, Rector, 28 West Twenty-second street; C. M. Wale, sexton, rear 159 West Thirtieth street.

Epiphany, 130 Stanton street; G. D. Smith, sexton, 110 Columbia street.

Good Shepherd, East Fifty-fourth street, near Second avenue; Ralph Hoyt, Rector, house at the church.

Grace, 800 Broadway; Thomas U. Taylor, Rector, 804 Broadway; Isaac H. Brown, sexton, 94 Fourth avenue.

Holy Apostles, Ninth avenue, corner of West Twenty-eighth street; R. S. Howland, Rector, 409 West Twenty-third street; G. J. Geer, Assistant, 229 West Twenty-seventh street; Robert Bennet, sexton, 230 Ninth avenue.

Holy Communion, Sixth avenue, corner of West Twentieth street; W. A. Muhlenberg, West Fifty-fourth street, corner of Fifth avenue, and F. E. Lawrence, 208 West Twentieth street, Pastors; J. E. Connor, sexton, 113 West Twentieth street.

Holy Innocents, 94 West Thirty-seventh street; John J. Elmendorf, Rector, 98 West Thirty-seventh street.

Holy Martyrs, 39 Forsyth street, J. Millett, Rector, 109 Second avenue; John J. Kearsing, sexton, 220½ Broome street.

Holy Trinity, Madison avenue, corner of East Forty-second S H. Tyng, Jr., Minister, 26 East Forty-first street; W. K. Whitford, sexton, 276 Sixth avenue.

Incarnation, East Thirty-fifth street, corner of Madison avenue; Henry E. Montgomery, Rector, 115 East Thirtieth street; William Lewers, sexton, 73 West Twenty-ninth street.

Intercession, West One Hundred and Fifty-fourth street, corner of Tenth avenue; J. H. Smith, Rector, West One Hundred and Fifty-sixth street, near Tenth avenue.

Madison Street Mission, 256 Madison street; W. A. Stirling, Minister, 58 Rutgers street.

Mediator, Lexington avenue, corner of East Thirtieth street; T. Irving, Minister; A. H. Langhans, sexton.

Memorial Church of the Rev. H. Anthon, 103 West Forty-eighth street; T. A. Jaggar, Minister; W. L. Childs, sexton, 744 Sixth avenue.

Messiah (colored,) 192 Mercer street.

Nativity, 70 Avenue C; Cabel Clapp, Rector, 225 Sixth street.

Our Saviour (floating,) foot of Pike street; Robert W. Lewis, Minister, 62 Pike street; John Williams, sexton.

Reconciliation, 150 East Thirty-first street ; ... S. Huntington, Minister : J. F. Hare, sexton.

Redeemer, East Eighty-fifth street, near Second avenue S. C. Thrall, Rector, 206 East Eighty-fourth street ; A. D. Ashmead, sexton, 1315 Third avenue.

Redemption, 98 East Fourteenth street ; R. G. Dickson, Minister, 91 East Thirteenth street John Green, sexton, 29 Third avenue.

Resurrection, 65 West Thirty-fifth street ; E. O. Flagg, Rector, 67 West Thirty-fifth street J. G. Burdett, sexton, 415 West Thirty-fourth street.

St. Alban's, Lexington avenue, corner Forty-seventh street ; C. W. Morrill,   inister ; B. McKeever, sexton, 736 Third avenue.

St. Andrew's, Harlem ; G. B. Draper, Rector, East One Hundred and Thirtieth street, near Fifth avenue.

St. Ann's, 7 West Eighteenth street ; Thomas Gallaudet, Rector, 9 West Eighteenth street ; E. Benjamin, Assistant, 164 East Thirteenth street ; S. M. Perine, sexton, 183 Third avenue.

St. Bartholomew's, Lafayette Place, corner Great Jones street ; S. Cooke, Rector, 60 West Eleventh street ; John Cantrell, sexton, 393 Fourth avenue.

St. Clement's, 108 Amity street ; T. A. Eaton, Rector, 106 West Thirteenth street ; Robert Heasley, sexton, 374 Bleecker street.

St. George's Chapel, Beekman street, corner Cliff street ; Sylvanus Reed, Minister ; J. Maret, sexton, 338 Pearl street.

St. George the Martyr, 39 West Forty-fourth street ; A. S. Leonard, Minister, 875 Broadway ; C. S. Hallock, sexton, 266 Eighth avenue.

St. George's, Rutherford Place, corner East Sixteenth street ; Stephen H. Tyng, Rector, 213 East Sixteenth street ; H. T. Tracy, Assistant ; George Briarly, sexton, 173 Third avenue. Mission Chapel, 220 East Nineteenth street ; C. S. Stephenson, Minister, 124 East Twenty-first street ; T. Tatley, sexton, at church.

St. George's German Chapel, East Fourteenth street, near First avenue ; C. Schramm, Minister, 91 Second street.

St. James, East Sixty-ninth street, near Third avenue ; P. S. Chauncey, Rector, 29 West Thirty-sixth street ; Edward L. Smith, sexton, 100 East Sixty-second street. Mission, East Eighty-fourth street, near Fourth avenue,

St. John Baptist, 231 Lexington avenue ; C. R. Duflie, Rector, 233 Lexington avenue ; E. Dowkers, sexton, 443 Third avenue.

St. John Evangelist, 20 Hammond street ; W. Coffman, sexton, 194 Waverly Place.

St. John's 46 Varick street ; S. H. Weston, 30 Laight street, and J. F. Young, 33½ West Twenty-fourth street, Ministers ; A. Craig, sexton, 17 Clarkson street.

St. Luke's, 483 Hudson street ; Isaac H. Tuttle, Rector, 477 Hudson street ; John M. Forbes, Assistant Minister, 7 Fifth avenue ; William Ely, sexton, 486 Hudson street.

St. Mark's, Stuyvesant street, near Second avenue ; A. H. Vinton, Rector, 156 Second avenue ; C. L. Carpenter, sexton, 24 Third avenue. Mission, 141 Avenue A ; G. W. Foote, Minister.

St. Mary's Manhattanville ; C. C. Adams, Rector.

St. Matthias', Broadway, corner West Thirty-second street ; N. E. Cornwall, Minister, 508 Seventh avenue.

St. Michael's, Broadway, corner West Ninety-ninth street ; T. McC. Peters, Rector, Broadway, corner West One Hundred and First street.

St. Paul's, Broadway, corner Vesey street ; B. J. Haight, Minister, 56 West Twenty-sixth street ; Henry Weld, sexton, 187 Fulton street.

St. Paul's, Harlem ; F. M. Serenbez, Minister.

St. Peter's, 224 West Twentieth street ; Alfred B. Beach, Rector, 228 West Twentieth street ; Robert Curran, Sexton, 169 Ninth avenue.

St. Philip's (colored,) 305 Mulberry street ; John Morgan, Minister, 762 Broadway ;'Charles Willets, sexton.

St. Saviour's, West Twenty-ninth street, near Ninth avenue ; G. L. Neide, Minister, 239 Ninth avenue.

St. Stephen's 120 Chrystie street ; J. H. Price, Rector, 62 Second avenue ; Henry R. Jones. sexton, 116 Chrystie street.

St. Thomas', Broadway, corner West Houston street; W. F. Morgan, Rector, Astoria ; Benjamin W. Williams, sexton, 276 Sixth avenue. Mission Chapel, 117 Thompson street; F. Sill, Minister, 25 Vandam street.

St. Timothy's, West Fifty-fourth street, near Eighth avenue ; G. J. Geer, Rector, 229 West Twenty-seventh street.

Transfiguration, East Twenty ninth street, near Fifth avenue ; G. H. Houghton, Rector, 1 East Twenty-ninth street ; J. C. Rappelyea, sexton, 414 Fourth avenue.

Trinity, Broadway, corner Rector street, and the Chapels of St. Paul's, St. John's, and Trinity Chapel ; Morgan Dix, Rector, 50 Varick street ; F. Vinton, Brooklyn, and F. Ogilby, 219 West Twenty third street, Assistant Ministers ; A. W. Meurer, sexton, Trinity church.

Trinity Chapel, 15 West Twenty-fifth street; E. Y. Higbee, 42 East Thirtieth street, and H. A. Neely, at church, Ministers ; Rutherford Clarke, sexton, 393 Fourth avenue.

Union (colored,) Second avenue, near East Eighty-fourth street.

Zion, Madison avenue, corner East Thirty-eight street; Horatio Southgate, Rector, 72 West Fortieth street; Alexander Samuels, sexton, 83 West Thirty-eighth street.

Zion Chapel, 557 Third avenue ; John Boyle, Minister, 179 East Forty-first street.

ROMAN CATHOLIC.

Annunciation B. V. M., West One Hundred and Thirty-first street, near Broadway ; John Breen, Priest.

Assumption, West Forty-ninth street, near Ninth avenue ; Benedict Strochle, Priest.

Holy Cross, 335 West Forty-second street ; Patrick McCarthy, Priest, 831 West Forty-second street ; Michael Hayes, sexton, 592 Eighth avenue.

Immaculate Conception, 245 East Fourteenth street; W. P. Morrogh, Priest, 243 East Fourteenth street.

Most Holy Redeemer, 165 Third street ; L. Petsch, Priest, 173 Third street ; J. Hoffman, sexton, 196 Third street.

Nativity, 46 Second avenue ; George McClosky, Priest, 44

Second avenue; Michael McGovern, sexton, 45 Second avenue.

St. Paul's, West Fifty-ninth street, near Ninth avenue; I. T. Hecker, Priest.

St. Alphonsus, 10 Thompson street; served from church of Most Holy Redeemer.

St. Andrew's Duane street, corner City Hall place; Michael Curran, Priest, 31 City Hall Place; T. Hamill, sexton, 17 City Hall place.

St. Ann's, 149 Eighth street; T. S. Preston, Priest, 145 Eighth street; M. Fox, sexton, at the church.

St. Boniface, East 47th street, near Second avenue; M. Nicot, Priest, 181 East Forty-seventh street.

St. Bridget's, Avenue B, corner of Eighth street; Thomas J. Mooney, Priest, 119 Avenue B; Isaac Brown, sexton, 1 Leandert's place.

St. Colomba's, 339 West Twenty-fifth street; M. McAleer, Priest, 343 West Twenty fifth street; Daniel Quinn, sexton, 333 West Twenty-fifth street.

St. Francis (German), 93 West Thirty-first street; A. Pfeiffer, Priest, 89 West Thirty-first street.

St. Francis Xavier, 36 West Sixteenth street; J. Loyzance, Priest, 49 West Fifteenth street; James Dowd, sexton, 119 West Eighteenth street.

St. Gabriel's, East Thirty-seventh street, near Second avenue; W. H. Clowry, Priest, 663 Second avenue.

St. James', 32 James street: J. Brennan, Priest, house 23 Oliver street.

St. John Baptist (German), 125 West Thirtieth street · Augustin Dantner, Priest, 127 West Thirtieth street.

St. John Evangelist, East Fiftieth street, near Fifth avenue; James McMahon, Priest, house near the church; J. Smith, sexton, 733 Third avenue.

St. Joseph's, Sixth avenue, corner of West Washington place; Thomas Farrell, Priest, 40 West Washington place; Nicholas Walsh, sexton, 8 Sixth avenue.

St Joseph's (German), West One Hundred and Twenty-fifth street, near Ninth avenue; F. A. Gerber, Priest.

St. Lawrence, East Eighty-fourth street, near Fourth avenue; S. Mulledy, Priest; T. Riley, sexton, East Eighty-third street, near Third avenue.

St. Mary's, 438 Grand street; Michael McCarron, Priest, 11 Ridge street; J. Terrell, sexton.

St. Michael's, 265 West Thirty-first street; Arthur J. Donnelly, Priest, 261 West Thirty-first street; J. McGee, sexton, 333 Ninth avenue.

St. Nicholas (German), 125 Second street; F. Krebez, Priest, 135 Second street.

St. Patrick's Cathedral, Mott street, corner of Prince street; Most Rev. John McCloskey, Archbishop; Very Rev. William Starrs, Vicar General; T. S. Preston, Chancellor; F. McNierny, Secretary; P. F. McSweeny, J. H. McGean, and Eugene Maguire, Priests; 263 Mulberry street; James Hart, sexton, 261 Mulberry street.

St Paul's, East One Hundred and Seventeenth street, near Fourth avenue; George R. Brophy Priest.

St. Peter's, Barclay street, corner of Church street; William Quinn, Priest, 15 Barclay street; Michael O'Meara, sexton, 70 North Moore street.

St. Stephen's, 93 East Twenty.eighth street; Rev. Dr. McGlynn, Priest, 80 East Twenty-ninth street; John McLaughlin, sexton.

St. Teresa, Rutgers street, corner of Henry street; James Boyce, Priest, 141 Henry street; Hugh Smith, sexton.

St. Vincent de Paul, 127 West Twenty-third street; Annet Lafont, Priest, 90 West Twenty-fourth street.

Transfiguration, Mott street, corner of Park street; Thomas Treanor, Priest, 30 Mott street.

UNITARIAN.

All Souls, Fourth avenue, corner East Twentieth street; H. W. Bellows, Minister, 59 East Twentieth street· Charles C. Simpson, sexton, 89 East Twenty-second street.

Messiah, East Twenty-eighth street, corner Madison avenue; S. Osgood, Minister, 154 West Eleventh street; James Berry, sexton, 619 Second avenue.

Third, West Fortieth street, near Sixth avenue; O. B. Fro-
thingham, Minister, 50 West Thirty-fifth street; S. P. Lathrop,
sexton, 602 Seventh avenue

UNIVERSALIST.

Second, East Eleventh street, corner Second avenue · G. L.
Demarest, Minister.
Third, 206 Bleecker street; G. R. Crary sexton, 17 St. Luke's
place.
Fourth, 548 Broadway, E. H. Chapin, Minister, 14 East
Thirty-third street; J. B. Ferdon, sexton, 82 Crosby street.
Sixth, 116 West Twentieth street; E. G. Brooks, Minister,
274 West Twenty fifth street.

MISCELLANEOUS.

Catholic Apostolic, 128 West Sixteenth street; D. M. Fackler,
Elder in charge, 216 West Twenty-fifth street.
Centre Street Mission, 110 Centre street
Christian Israelites, 108 First street; J. L. Bishop, Minister,
108 First street.
Church of the True Believers, Levi Rightmyer, Treasurer.
Disciples' Meeting House, 24 West Twenty-eighth street;
E. Parmly and Dani 1 Monroe, Elders; Urban C. Brewer, Min-
ister, 25 East Thirty-first street.
Evangelical, rear 108 West Twenty-fourth street; C. B.
Fliehr, Minister, at church.
First Congregational Methodist, West Twenty-fourth street,
near Sixth avenue; Samuel Curry, Minister, 189 West Twenty-
ninth street.
German Evangelical Reformed, 97 Suffolk street; J. F.
Busche, Minister 108 Rivington street.
Mariners', Madison street, corner Catherine street; E. D.
Murphy, Minister, 72 Madison street; Thomas Halverson, sex-
ton, at church.
Messiah's, 7 Seventh avenue; P Hawkes, Minister, at church.
St. John's (Ind.) Methodist Church, 10 West Forty-first
street; D. Hand, sexton, at church.
Second Advent, 68 East Broadway; G. Storrs, Minister.

Seventh-Day Baptist, Second avenue, corner East Eleventh street.

Swedenborgian First New Church Society, 68 East Thirty fifth street ; Chauncey Giles, Minister, 43 East Thirty-third street.

True Reformed Dutch, 25 King street: John Demott, sexton.

United Brethren (Moravian,) J. H. Kummer, Minister, 51 East Houston street.

Welsh Methodist Calvinistic, 133 East Thirteenth street; William Roberts, Minister, 204 East Sixteenth street ; Thomas Jones, sexton, 194 East Thirteenth steeet.

Wesleyan Methodist Church of the Pilgrims, 235 West Forty-eighth street ; Seymour A. Baker, Minister, house next to church.

MISSIONS.

CITY MISSIONS.—27 Greenwich street; 147 Duane street; 327 Madison street; 593 Hudson street; 21 Avenue D; 39 Columbia street; 22½ Marion street; Fifth street, corner of First avenue ; 283 Avenue B; 176 West Thirty-seventh street; 555 First avenue ; corner Fourth street and Avenue C.

PROTESTANT EPISCOPAL CITY MISSIONS.—304 Mulberry street.

METHODIST EPISCOPAL MISSIONS.—21 Worth street ; 289 Rivington street; 117 Bank street ; Fourth street, corner of Avenue C ; Tenth avenue, near Thirty-seventh street; Ninth avenue, near Fifty-fourth street.

Hours of service on the Lord's day, 10½ A.M., 3½ and 7½ P.M. Sabbath school, 9 A.M., and 2 P.M. Week-day evening services generally on Tuesday and Friday evenings, 7½ o'clock.

Noon-day Prayer-meeting, Consistory Room, Fulton street, near William street, daily, from 12 to 1 o'clock. Daily Prayers in Trinity Protestant Episcopal church. Daily Prayer-meeting, Mariner's Church, 72 Madison street. Young Men's Christian Association—rooms open day and evening—161 Fifth avenue, corner of Twenty-second street.

Strangers visiting the city, desiring information as to the Churches, the Missions, or any of the Religious or Charitable Institutions, can obtain it at the rooms of the New York City Mission, 30 Bible-house, Third avenue.

HINTS FOR REFERENCE

CARRIAGE FARES.

Not exceeding one mile, one passenger, 50 cents; each additional passenger, 37½ cents. Exceeding one mile, and not exceeding two miles, one passenger, 75 cents; each additional passenger, 37½ cents. Children under two years of age, no charge; between two and fourteen, half price only is to be charged. The baggage to be taken without charge with each passenger, is one trunk, valise, saddle-bag, carpet-bag, portmanteau or box, if he be requested so to do; but for any trunk or other such article above named, more than one for each passenger, six cents can be charged. No charge can be made unless the number of the carriage is placed on the outside, and the rates of fare in a conspicuous place inside of said carriage. If more than the legal rates are asked, nothing can be collected for services. A violation of this ordinance subjects the offender to a fine of $10.

TO WHICH IS ADDED A TABLE OF DISTANCES.

Fm Battery.	Exch'ge.	City Hall.	To
¼ mile			.....Rector street.
½	¼ mile		.....Fulton street.
¾	½		.....City Hall.
1	¾	¼ mile	.....Leonard street.
1¼	1	½	.....Canal street.
1½	1¼	¾	.....Spring street.
1¾	1½	1	.....Houston street.
2	1¾	1¼	.....Fourth street.
2¼	2	1½	.....Ninth street.
2½	2¼	1¾	.....Fourteenth street.
2¾	2½	2	....Nineteenth street.
3	2¾	2¼	.....Twenty-fourth street
3¼	3	2½	....Twenty-ninth street.
3½	3¼	2¾	.....Thirty-fourth street.
3¾	3½	3	.....Thirty-eighth street.
4	3¾	3¼	.....Forty-fourth street.
4¼	4	3½	.....Forty-ninth street.
4½	4¼	3¾	....Fifty-fourth street.
4¾	4½	4	.... Fifty-eighth street.
5	4¾	4¼	.....Sixty-third street.
5¼	5	4½	.....Sixty-eighth street.
5½	5¼	4¾	.....Seventy-third street.
5¾	5½	5	.....Seventy-eighth street.
6	5¾	5¼	.....Eighty-third street
6¼	6	5½	.....Eighty-eighth street.
6½	6¼	5¾	.....Ninety-third street.
6¾	6½	6	.....Ninety-seventh street.
7	6¾	6¼	.....One Hundred and Second street.
7¼	7	6½	....One Hundred and Seventh street.
7½	7¼	6¾	.....One Hundred and Twelfth street.
7¾	7½	7	.....One Hundred and Seventeenth street.
8	7¾	7¼	.....One Hundred and Twenty-first street.
8¼	8	7½	.....One Hundred and Twenty-sixth street.

BANKS.

Banks marked with an asterisk are under the State system; all others are National.

American.........80 Broadway	Leather M'frs..........29 Wall
Am. Exch.......128 Broadway	Manhattan Co*.........40 Wall
Atlantic.........142 Broadway	Manufacturers....... 132 Front
Bk. of America*........46 Wall	Manuf. & Merch*..561 Broadway
Bk. of the Republic......2 Wall	Market....... ......286 Pearl
Bk. of New York. .....48 Wall	Marine................90 Wall
Bk. of N. America......44 Wall	Mechanics'............33 Wall
Bk. of Commonwealth.15 Nassau	Mech. Bk'g Ass'n........38 Wall
Bk. of Commerce.....29 Nassau	Mech. & Traders'.. 153 Bowery
Bowery.............58 Bowery	Mercantile.......191 Broadway
Bk. of St. of N. Y....33 William	Merch'ts Ex .....257 Broadway
Broadway........237 Broadway	Metropolitan.....108 Broadway
Bull's Head*......314 Third Av	Merchants.............42 Wall
Butchers' & Drovers'.124 Bowery	Nassau*............137 Nassau
Central.........318 Broadway	Nat'l Currency.........2 Wall
Chatham........182 Broadway	N. Y. County......81 Eighth Av
Chemical.......270 Broadway	N. Y. Exchange..185 Greenwich
Citizens'.........381 Broadway	North River* ....187 Greenwich
City..............52 Wall	Ninth...........363 Broadway
Continental...........7 Nassau	Ocean........ .197 Greenwich
Corn Exch*.........13 William	Oriental*..........122 Bowery
Croton.............17 Nassau	Park ....5 Beekman
Dry Dock*..........143 Av. D	Pacific..........470 Broadway
East River ....680 Broadway	People's*...........395 Canal
Eighth..........650 Broadway	Phœnix...............45 Wall
Fifth.............338 Third Av	St. Nicholas............7 Wall
First.............140 Broadway	Second...........190 Fifth Av
Fourth................27 Pine	Seventh Ward........234 Pearl
Fulton ....37 Fulton	Shoe & Leather...271 Broadway
Gallatin.....:........36 Wall	Sixth......Broadway cor. 35th
Greenwich*........402 Hudson	Tenth...........240 Broadway
Grocers'...........59 Barclay	Third...............25 Nassau
Hanover............33 Nassau	Tradesmen's .....291 Broadway
Imp. & Traders'...247 Broadway	Union.................34 Wall
Irving.....Warren & Greenwich	

INSURANCE OFFICES.

FIRE.

Adriatic.........139 Broadway	Astor................16 Wall
Ætna†..........170 Broadway	Atlantic, Brooklyn.....14 Wall
Ætna (Hartford).......62 Wall	American†.......... 48 Wall
Arctic.............18 Wall	Am. Exchange ...141 Broadway

Baltic................54 Wall
Beekman..............10 Wall
Broadway.......158 Broadway
Brooklyn, Brooklyn.....18 Wall
Central Park.....168 Broadway
Citizens'.........156 Broadway
City.................58 Wall
Clinton.........156 Broadway
Columbia†......161 Broadway
Commercial...........49 Wall
Commonwealth...151 Broadway
Continental......102 Broadway
Corn Exchange...157 Broadway
Commerce.............27 Wall
Croton.........180 Broadway
Eagle.................71 Wall
East River.............69 Wall
Empire City......102 Broadway
Equitable, N. Y........58 Wall
Excelsior........130 Broadway
Exchange........170 Broadway
Firemen's........153 Broadway
Firemen's Fund...200 Broadway
Firemen's Trust........52 Wall
Franklin, Philadelphia...27 Wall
Fulton..........172 Broadway
Gallatin..........96 Broadway
Gebhard.........141 Broadway
Germania........175 Broadway
Globe...........197 Greenwich
Greenwich.......155 Broadway
Grocers'..............76 Wall
Guardian........142 Broadway
Hamilton.............11 Wall
Harmony........158 Broadway
Hanover.............45 Wall
Hoffman.........161 Broadway
Home...........135 Broadway
Hope.............92 Broadway
Howard...............66 Wall
Humboldt.......140 Broadway
Irving...............9 Wall
Imp's & Traders..100 Broadway
International.....113 Broadway
Indemnity........207 Broadway
Jefferson............60 Wall

Jersey City, N. J.......67 Wall
Kings Co., Brooklyn...1 Nassau
Knickerbocker.........64 Wall
Lamar................50 Wall
Lenox..............16 Wall
Liverpool & London..45 William
Lorillard†........104 Broadway
Long Island...........48 Wall
LaFayette, Brooklyn....14 Wall
Manhattan.............68 Wall
Market................37 Wall
Mechanics', Brooklyn...31 Wall
Mechanics & Traders....48 Wall
Mercantile.......165 Broadway
Merchants'.......106 Broadway
Metropolitan†....108 Broadway
Montauk, Brooklyn..168 B'dway
Nassau, Brooklyn......65 Wall
National..............52 Wall
New Amsterdam.......20 Wall
N. Y. Fire & Marine....72 Wall
Niagara..............12 Wall
N. American†....114 Broadway
North River.....202 Greenwich
New World......151 Broadway
Pacific..........470 Broadway
Park............237 Broadway
People's.........157 Broadway
Peter Cooper..........74 Wall
Phœnix, Brooklyn.139 Broadway
Republic†.......153 Broadway
Rutgers..........130 Chatham
Relief................8 Wall
Resolute†........151 Broadway
Sterling.........155 Broadway
St. Mark's............67 Wall
St. Nicholas......166 Broadway
Stuyvesant.........122 Bowery
Security†........119 Broadway
Standard..............11 Wall
Star............187 Greenwich
Tradesmen's......153 Bowery
United States..........69 Wall
Washington......172 Broadway
Williamsburg City.165 Broadway
Yonkers & N. Y..161 Broadway

† Participation.

150 HINTS FOR REFERENCE.

LIFE INSURANCE.

American Mutual..170 Broadway	Mutual..........146 Broadway
Equitable........92 Broadway	New York.......112 Broadway
Germania........90 Broadway	N. E. Mutual.....110 Broadway
Knickerbocker...121 Broadway	North America......63 William
Life & Travelers'..243 Broadway	Security...,..........31 Pine
Manhattan.......156 Broadway	Washington.......98 Broadway

MARINE INSURANCE.

Atlantic Mutual........51 Wall	Orient Mutual..........43 Wall
Com. Mutual........57 William	Pacific Mutual....111 Broadway
Gr. Western.........39 William	Security.........119 Broadway
Metropolitan.....103 Broadway	Sun Mutual.............49 Wall
Mercantile Mutual......35 Wall	Union Mutual.......61 William
N. Y. Mutual........61 William	Washington Mutual.....40 Pine

POST OFFICE GUIDE.

The Post Office opens at 7.30 A. M., and closes at 7 P. M. On Sundays, open from 9 to 10 A. M., and 12.30 to 1.30 P. M. Letters obtained at any hour of the night at the night window on Nassau street.

MAILS CLOSE.

North Through, 5 A. M.; 3.45 P. M.
North Way, 2 P. M.
Harlem Railroad, 5.30 A. M.
East (via New Haven), 5 A. M.; 1.30, 6 P. M.
East (New Haven Way), 2.20 P. M.
East (via Newport), 4 P. M.
South, 5 A. M.; 4.30, 5.30, 10.30 P. M.
Erie Railroad, 5 A. M.; 4.15 P. M. Way, 5 A. M.; 3 P. M.
New York Central, 3 P. M.
New Jersey Central, 5 A. M.; 2 P. M.
New Jersey Northern, 2.30 P. M.
Morris & Essex, 5 A. M.; 2 P. M.
Freehold and Keyport, 1.30 P. M.
Staten Island, 5 A. M.; 2 P. M.
Brooklyn, 5, 9 A. M.; 2, 4.30 P. M.
Astoria, 9 A. M.; 3.30 P. M. Long Island, 5 A. M.; 2½ P. M.
Mineola, Hempstead, Jamaica, Syosset, 5 A. M.; 2.30 P. M.
Canada East (except Fridays), 5 A. M.; 3.45 P. M.
Canada East (Fridays) 5 A. M.; 6 P. M.
Canada West, 5 A. M.; 6.45 P. M.
California, (overland,) 5 A M.; 4.15 P. M.
Atlanta, Augusta, (Ga.,) Charleston, Columbus, (Miss.,) Mobile, Montgomery, (Ala.,) New Orleans, Pensacola, Wilmington, (N.C.,) 5 A. M. Richmond, 5 A. M.; 5.30 P. M.
SUNDAYS, ALL MAILS CLOSE AT 1.30 P. M.

www.ingramcontent.com/pod-product-compliance
Lightning Source LLC
Chambersburg PA
CBHW020544270326
41927CB00006B/707

* 9 7 8 3 7 4 4 7 5 5 7 8 8 *